SO MUCH MORE

A Spiritual Blueprint For Building
the Life Your Soul Longs For

CHARITY CRAIG

AMOR DIVINUS PRESS

For permissions, inquiries, or media requests, contact:

Amor Divinus Press

www.amordivinuspress.com

info@amordivinuspress.com

ISBN 979-8-9937492-0-4

Printed in the United States of America

To the One who whispered, "My dove."

CONTENTS

AN INVITATION

You don't have to read this book in a weekend.

In fact, I hope you don't.

We live in a society that rushes everything. We measure progress by how quickly we finish, but the most meaningful experiences rarely happen that way.

If we pay attention, creation itself shows us another rhythm.

Nature teaches us the wisdom of slow cycles. The seasons change in their time, the tides rise and fall at their own pace, and the sun sets and rises again without hurry.

I wrote this book with that same rhythm in mind.

The twenty-eight chapters reflect the quiet cadence of a woman's monthly cycle and the phases of the moon. This structure is a gentle reminder that transformation unfolds in its own time, deepens with each season, and often circles back again and again.

This isn't a book to consume quickly and check off your

list. It's not a race to the final page. It's an invitation to slow your pace, sit with the words, and let them breathe.

You might read one chapter a day.

You might linger on a single paragraph for a week.

You might return to the same page months from now and discover something entirely new.

There's no prize for finishing fast.

Each chapter is a stone. Each idea is meant to be held, turned over, and examined in the light of your own life.

If you try to devour this book in one sitting, you may miss its depth. Instead, allow it to move with you, shaping something sacred within.

So take your time.

Read slowly.

Pause often.

Return again and again.

Let this be an invitation to enter a new, unrushed rhythm.

Charity Craig
March 2026

WHY A CATHEDRAL

Cathedrals are the visible expressions of the human spirit reaching toward God. They're the outer reflections of humanity's deepest desire to build a dwelling place for the Divine. Their spires rise like prayers carved in stone, and their arches curve as if forming holy portals between heaven and earth.

Step inside one of these sacred spaces, and something within you instinctively softens. The air hums with reverence. Sunlight filters through stained glass, scattering color across ancient floors, and in that stillness, you feel the quiet awareness that God is near.

Even though cathedrals are associated with Catholicism, their essence transcends religion. They represent our soul's universal hunger to know and be with God. Every chime of a bell is humanity's way of declaring, *There is more to this life.*

For centuries, builders have dedicated their lives to erecting sanctuaries that reflect the grandeur of God. The architecture and awe of cathedrals remind us of what it means to worship with our whole being. They're the physical embodiment of humanity's faith.

Even as they rise in majesty, cathedrals don't contain God, because the Divine can't be confined to stone or glass. The truth is that God's dwelling place has never been a building, but a being.

I chose the cathedral because it captures something your heart already understands without needing explanation. A cathedral is not thrown together. It's imagined, designed, labored over, and built stone by stone. It requires vision, patience, sacrifice, and faith that what's unseen will one day stand in beauty. That's exactly what a meaningful life requires.

Everything about this book is meant to give you a foundation to make something beautiful and sacred with your life. Human beings ache to matter. We want our years here to mean something. We want to leave behind more than noise and busyness. And what greater structure could symbolize that longing than a cathedral? It holds together sacred beauty, eternal purpose, and divine connection all in one image.

As you turn these pages, I hope something stirs in you. I hope the outline of your cathedral slowly emerges from the fog of the forgotten corners of your soul.

May you see that your life isn't random, and that you're not here to drift or disappear. There's something sacred within you waiting to take form, something beautiful that only your hands can build.

You're building something sacred.

It's time to get to work.

PART 1

YOUR LIFE IS A CATHEDRAL

PURPOSE

1

———————————

THE ACHE FOR MORE

PRAYER

"Thank You for the gift of life. Teach me to build something beautiful with it."

The Ache for More in Life

Take a deep breath and exhale. Now, take another one, but slower. Pause for a few moments and pay attention to your chest as it rises and falls. Do you feel it? That movement is life, and it's your extraordinary gift. What's strange about it is that none of us know exactly what we're supposed to do with our gift. There isn't a clear, step-by-step playbook for us to follow.

Even though we're not always clear on the purpose of our lives, we sense that it's not enough to exist. Your soul longs to live beyond daily struggle and the endless striving just to make it through. There's a stirring under the surface, a desire for so much more. It's not enough to be born, struggle as you circle the sun several dozen times, and die.

You want your life to mean something, to wake up each day excited and alive. You desire a life that feels so beautiful and so full that you never need a vacation to escape it.

Jesus said, "I have come that they may have life, and have it more abundantly." Two thousand years later, those words still cut through the noise. They make your heart skip a beat as your soul whispers, *Maybe, just maybe, there's more for me.*

Your ache for more is your soul reaching for the abundant life Jesus promised. You've been reaching since the Divine breathed life into you. You can feel it and long to fulfill it. Your desire for more isn't selfishness or greed. It's God Himself seeking to express Himself through you.

Over a century ago, Wallace Wattles captured this idea in a way that still rings true today. In *The Science of Getting Rich*, he wrote:

> "God…is trying to live and do and enjoy things
> through humanity. He is saying, 'I want hands to
> build wonderful structures, to play divine harmonies,
> to paint glorious pictures; I want feet to run my
> errands, eyes to see my beauties, tongues to tell
> mighty truths and to sing marvelous songs,' and
> so on."

If that language stirs something in you, it's because it echoes a much older truth.

Long before Wattles put words to it, Jesus told a story that defined humanity's role in this divine partnership. He described a master preparing for a journey who entrusted his servants with his wealth. One received five talents, another two, and the last received one.

While the master was away, the first two invested their talents and doubled them. The third, afraid of failing, buried his single talent in the ground. When the master returned, he was pleased with the first two but heartbroken over the last, calling him wicked and lazy.

The third servant wasn't reprimanded because he was given little or returned little. His master was disappointed because the servant refused to participate. He buried what was given him and returned it exactly as he received it, untouched and unchanged.

You were given a talent too: your life, and its purpose is to multiply it.

You didn't ask for your life, and you didn't choose its starting point. You can't control every circumstance that shapes it, but you're still its steward.

Whether you were given five talents or one, whether your beginning feels abundant or unfair, that isn't what determines the success of your life. It's what you build with it that matters.

Every day you wake up and go to work so you can put food on the table and keep a roof over your head. You cook meals, pay bills, fold laundry, answer emails, and care for your family. This is the weight of being human. There's no skipping it.

These tasks sustain your body. They keep you safe and warm, but survival alone doesn't satisfy your soul.

Doubling your talents doesn't mean escaping your responsibilities. It's not about moving off to a foreign country to do mission work or lounging on a beach drinking piña coladas. You don't need to abandon the ordinary work of your days, but instead transform it.

Your daily tasks themselves aren't what give you purpose, but the meaning you attach to them. The same work can feel heavy or holy depending on the vision behind it.

To see what I mean, imagine two stone masons working side by side.

The Tale of Two Masons

A man came across two masons who were working at chipping chunks of granite from large blocks. The first seemed unhappy at his job, chipping away and frequently looking at his watch. When the man asked what it was that he was doing, the first mason responded, rather curtly, "I'm hammering this stupid rock, and I can't wait 'til I can go home."

The second mason was hammering at his block fervently, taking time to stand back and admire his work. He chipped off small pieces until he was satisfied that it was the best he could do. When questioned about the work, he stopped, gazed skyward, and proudly proclaimed, "I am building a cathedral." (Author Unknown)

You're a stone mason in life, and your purpose is to build a cathedral.

You spend every day grinding, trying to make a life for

yourself, but you're only surviving unless you work with purpose.

The only difference between the two masons was their perspective. They were both hammering at stones, but they had two entirely different experiences. One was chipping, the other was building. One was surviving, the other was expanding, and it all came down to the meaning and purpose they gave their work.

You weren't created to eat, sleep, and repeat until time runs out. The work of our hands is meant to serve something far greater. We are meant to expand our lives. Every task, no matter how small, can become sacred when you shift your perspective and see its greater purpose.

Expand in All Areas

Abundance isn't limited to finances or career success. It's built into every dimension of your life: mental, emotional, spiritual, and relational.

Just as the walls of a cathedral must be strong enough to support the roof, and the stained glass windows depend on the frames to hold them in place, every area of your life depends on all other aspects of your life. A crack in one corner eventually affects the entire structure.

You can't have one area of your life suffer without causing all areas to suffer.

When your thoughts are filled with fear, your creativity is blocked. When your body is exhausted, your spirit feels distant. When resentment lingers in your heart, your relationships suffer. Everything is connected.

Building your cathedral is all-encompassing. God is all-encompassing, and your fulfillment of his purpose means all areas of your life. Abundant living means your mind, body, finances, and relationships will expand.

Don't ignore the burning desire for more in all areas. That ache did not appear by accident. It's not a flaw in your character or a sign that you're ungrateful for what you have. It's the whisper of eternity placed in your heart. It's the evidence that you were made to expand.

Open yourself up to the possibility that the longing you feel is an invitation to build a life with more depth, more beauty, and more impact.

Your purpose isn't a secret assignment or a riddle to solve. It's not hidden in the heavens waiting for revelation. It's simple and universal: take what God gave you and multiply it.

So here you are, feet on the ground, hammer in hand. The work is in front of you.

Will you chip at rocks or build a cathedral?

AFFIRMATION

"I'm building a cathedral."

2

____

HOW TO FULFILL YOUR PURPOSE

PRAYER

"Open my inner eyes that I may see Your will clearly."

____

What Does God Want Me to Build?

We can now see that your purpose is to expand your life. You're not here to scrape by, but to build an abundant cathedral. Our shared, collective purpose is to take the life God has given us and multiply it.

That often leads to more questions. *How do I do that? How does God actually want me to build my cathedral?*

Building something with your life sounds beautiful, but it's also wide open. There are a million different ways a life can expand. It could be in business, motherhood, art, teaching, healing, creating, leading, and the list goes on.

This is where many people get stuck. When the possibilities feel endless, you can feel overwhelmed. Too many options, combined with the fear of getting it wrong, create paralysis. Instead of moving forward, you get stuck circling the same mountain, asking the same questions, waiting for clarity that never seems to come.

As a person of faith, the hesitation can feel even heavier. You don't want to build just anything. You want God's will, so you wait, overanalyze, and pray for signs. You live in constant indecision, hoping one day the path will become unmistakably clear.

Much of our fear and hesitation comes from confusion, and we fear what we don't understand. We use spiritual language like, *finding God's purpose.* Or, *doing God's will.* These phrases can feel vague, and when something feels too abstract, it's easy to doubt yourself and God. And when you doubt, you delay.

To help you overcome your fear and indecision, I want to pause and clarify what these phrases mean, so you can begin building with confidence.

God's Will vs. Your Purpose

We talk about God's will and God's purpose as the same thing, and in many ways they're closely connected, but I want to slow down and gently separate them, so that the fog can begin to lift.

We've already explored your purpose. It's the broad, shared calling written into every human life: to expand and multiply what you've been given.

Your purpose is the great why behind your existence. Every person carries this same blueprint. We're here to take our gifts, our time, and our abilities and build something meaningful with them.

God's will is different.

If purpose is the *why*, God's will is the *how*.

It's the spirit in which you build. It's the posture of your heart as you expand. It shapes how you make decisions, how you treat people, and how you move through your work and your seasons.

Your purpose answers the question, *What am I here for?*

God's will answers, *How do I live it out?*

Now it's time to lean in and explore God's will for your life.

Understanding God's Will

Just as our purpose is collective for humanity, so is God's will.

God's will for my life is the same as God's will for yours.

We've been taught to imagine God's will as a private, hidden file locked in heaven with our name on it, and if we pray hard enough, He'll drop it down to us, but Jesus never taught it that way. He made it very simple to know God's will when He reduced it to two commands:

1. Love God with your whole being.
2. Love your neighbor as yourself.

That's God's will here on earth: Love God, others, and yourself.

When you look at the two commandments, what is the common thread in both? Love.

Our purpose is to expand, and the way we expand is through Love. Love is the channel. Love is the foundation. Love is the energy that turns ordinary into sacred.

Now, this doesn't immediately answer the question, should I start the business? Or is this the right move? We'll get to the practical steps for answering these later, but before you decide what to build, you must understand how to build.

Whenever you need to make a decision, and you're wondering if it's God's will, ask yourself one question: Is this rooted in Love?

Does it grow Love in you?

Does it extend Love through you?

If the answer is yes, you're in God's will.

You don't need a secret revelation. You need alignment.

Alignment matters because you can expand your life and still miss God's will.

Missing God's Will

You can build, achieve, and accumulate without being in God's will. You can multiply money, status, or influence, and from the outside, it appears to be expansion. It looks impressive.

But not all expansion is rooted in Love.

There's a kind of expansion that's rooted in fear. Fear of not being enough. Fear of being forgotten. Fear of not mattering. This kind of expansion pushes, hustles, and strives, trying to quiet the inner ache for more.

That kind of growth isn't true expansion. It's bloat.

Bloat swells quickly, but it isn't healthy. It's driven by selfish ambition, greed, or the need to prove something. It may increase your external world, but internally, you're lacking. The more you gain, the more anxious you become. The more you achieve, the more you fear losing it. It looks big, but it doesn't last. It demands constant striving to sustain it.

True growth aligned with God's will feels different.

When you expand in Love, it carries a distinct fruit. It produces peace in the middle of chaos. It brings confidence without arrogance. It fosters kindness, patience, and steadiness. Even when the work is hard, there's a quiet anchor inside you. You're not frantic. You're not grasping. You're building from fullness, not from lack.

We'll explore the character of Love more deeply in a later chapter. But even now, you already know the difference.

Growth rooted in Love feels grounded. Growth rooted in fear feels urgent.

Growth rooted in Love brings freedom. Growth rooted in fear brings captivity.

When you learn to recognize the fruit, the confusion clears. You begin to see that not all expansion is equal, and when you know the difference, you can choose the kind of growth that fulfills your deepest desire.

Your Unique Expression of God's Will

God's will doesn't change from person to person. He's not telling one person, "Love God. Love people," and another, "Hoard. Isolate. Self-promote."

The assignment beneath it all is the same: expand in Love.

How Love takes shape in your life is where the beauty begins.

God's will is universal. Your expression of it is not.

The way you embody Love, the gifts you carry, and the creativity you foster are uniquely yours. Love may be the foundation, but the structure that rises from it will look different for every person.

This is where your cathedral becomes personal.

How you express Love will evolve. It'll stretch you, refine you, and take on new forms in different chapters of your life, but the heartbeat remains the same: Love expanding through you.

Like many Christians, I spent most of my life trying to figure out God's will as if it were a hidden map I hadn't earned the right to see. I wandered. I survived. I did mom-life. I did church. I did whatever was in front of me. But I felt lost, constantly wondering, *Am I doing the thing God wants me to do?*

After walking through one of the darkest chapters of my life, I experienced a transformation that set my soul on fire, and, with new clarity, I knew I was meant to help women rebuild their lives and marriages. It felt sacred, clear, and divine.

For the first time, I felt like I had found God's will.

But one afternoon, sitting in the school pickup line, grief unexpectedly washed over me. I felt a deep sadness as I began to question why it took me going through hell to discover God's will for my life. Did my life not have purpose until now?

I remembered a gala my husband and I attended for a nonprofit that gives one final vacation to families before a terminally ill parent passes. The organization was born from a man's crushing grief after losing his wife. His pain became purpose, and it was beautiful.

But as I sat in my car, I wondered: *Did his life only start counting after tragedy? Or did God have a purpose for him before the loss?*

And that's when it clicked for me.

God's will wasn't revealed in the crisis. It expanded there. Our purpose to grow and multiply with Love is always present throughout life.

What changes is the expression of it.

Before my crisis, I was a young wife and mother, building a home and nurturing little souls. That was God's will. It was Love.

Now I help women heal their marriages and rediscover themselves. That's also God's will. Also Love.

Same purpose. Different expression.

Every season hands you a new way to build in Love.

It may look like raising babies in the quiet hours of the morning. It may look like serving your community, showing up faithfully to a 9–5, or caring for aging parents. None of it is small when it's rooted in Love.

So stop waiting for God to reveal some hidden assignment. He's not withholding His will. He's waiting for you.

Go and in your own unique way, expand in Love. Let Love move through your hands, your voice, your work, and your home. Let it shape what you build and how you build it.

The world needs your cathedral.

AFFIRMATION

"My purpose is to expand in Love and allow Love to expand through me."

3

THE SACRED YES

PRAYER

"Meet me in my yes, as I join You in this sacred partnership."

Chapel of the Madonna di Vitaleta

Tucked away in the rolling hills of Tuscany is the little Chapel of the Madonna di Vitaleta. It's easy to miss unless you step off the main road and walk a dirt path roughly a mile through wheat fields and cypress trees.

Since its construction in the late 16th century, despite its small size, the light-stoned chapel has become one of Tuscany's most iconic and most photographed locations. Although it doesn't tower over a city or host massive crowds, its presence is felt by anyone who pauses to witness its expression of eternity.

The Chapel of the Madonna di Vitaleta doesn't compete with Rome's grand cathedrals. It doesn't dominate a skyline or command a crowd. And yet, it makes a meaningful impact on the world.

Its purpose isn't expressed in its size or grandeur, but in its purpose and contribution.

Somewhere inside you, there may be a quiet comparison that whispers, *Is my life enough? If I don't build something grand and visible, will my small and unseen life mean anything?*

The little chapel in Tuscany answers that fear without ever speaking a word.

Some cathedrals rise high and reshape cities. Others sit quietly in fields. Neither is lesser. Both are sacred.

Should I Build Grand or Small?

No two cathedrals in history are identical. Each carries its own architecture, its own light, and its own story carved into stone. In the same way, your life is meant to rise according to your design.

For some people, their gifts and the fire within them will lead them to build a vast cathedral that rises high, dominating the landscape around them. These people are household names that fill history books and inspire movements. Like Notre Dame or St. Peter's Basilica, their impact is widespread.

These are the thinkers who stretch minds, the inventors who change the way we live, the leaders who move nations, and the artists whose work stirs the human soul. Their cathedrals stand in public view, admired and remembered. Their work matters because it expands humanity, moving the collective closer to God.

You may build a life that carries your name beyond your lifetime, filling books and inspiring generations. If that's you, don't shrink back from it. Build boldly.

Just as sacred and just as necessary are the lives that never dominate skylines or headlines. Their quiet presence in the back hills of society leaves an imprint on every heart they touch. The mothers, teachers, friends, and neighbors who pour Love into ordinary places may never have books written about them, but their influence ripples through generations.

Both are sacred. Both are important.

Maybe thinking about how big you're going to build your life doesn't clear things up for you. Maybe you feel just as overwhelmed and just as uncertain.

It doesn't matter if your cathedral is a vast structure or a simple chapel. Don't worry so much about the size of your life, because what matters is that you and God are co-creating together. What makes it holy isn't how many people admire it, but that it reflects Love.

God rarely hands us the entire plan at once. He usually invites you to begin before you can see the whole picture. It's less like unrolling the blueprint and more like opening a puzzle and spreading the pieces across the table. At first, the image isn't clear, but as you keep working piece by piece, the picture slowly begins to appear.

As you work side by side with God, the path becomes clearer, the pieces begin to fit, and the blueprint gradually reveals itself.

You don't need a perfect plan to begin. You only need a sacred yes.

Start With a Sacred Yes

Every puzzle begins with a yes. Not a detailed plan. Not a five-year vision. Just a simple, wholehearted yes to God's invitation to build something with Him.

The posture of yes is one of the most powerful positions you can take in life. It doesn't mean you have everything figured out or that you've mapped out the details. Yes is simply a willing heart with a courageous openness that invites the Divine to move through you.

Yes shifts you from control to trust. You stop demanding to see the entire blueprint and instead allow His light to illuminate your feet as you walk.

The moment you posture your heart in willingness, heaven responds. The Divine begins aligning opportunities, people, and ideas to guide you toward what's meant for you.

A yes doesn't remove uncertainty. It transforms it. It turns fear into curiosity and hesitation into momentum. Your willingness to join the divine partnership tells God, *I'm ready to build with You, even if I don't yet see the full design.*

Say yes to the truth that whatever you build with Love is sacred. Yes to the reality that your cathedral is yours alone to build. Yes to the promise that even the smallest stone, if laid with intention, will matter.

You don't need the final form today. You only need to say yes to the work in front of you.

Seek with Childlike Curiosity

Once you say yes, the next step isn't to sit back and wait. It's to become a seeker.

Jesus said we must be like little children to enter the kingdom of God. What makes children worthy of the kingdom isn't their perfection or knowledge, but their unfiltered curiosity. Children don't wait until they understand everything before they move. They live in wonder. They ask questions. They reach for what they don't yet understand without shame or ego. They explore because something pulls them forward.

This is the posture of a builder.

When you bring that same childlike curiosity into your life, your yes becomes a quest. You stop demanding immediate answers and begin seeking them. You lean in instead of holding back. You pay attention. You notice how life whispers through desires that won't leave you alone, through unexpected opportunities, and through holy nudges that stir something deep inside.

Jesus told us how to be childlike by giving us the pattern: ask, seek, and knock.

He didn't say 'wait' passively or 'freeze' in fear. He didn't ask you to bury what you've been given.

He said, "Ask. Seek. Knock."

Your role in discovering what and how you must build your cathedral is active participation. When you're open and engaged, what once felt impossible becomes possible. Provision is given when you ask. Opportunities are found when you seek. Doors open when you knock.

Become like a little child with your yes. Ask more questions. Follow what feels alive and explore what's aligned with

Love. It's through the steady rhythm of asking, seeking, and knocking that the design of your cathedral becomes clear.

Your sacred yes is only the start. Now your lifelong work begins.

AFFIRMATION

"Big or small, my cathedral is holy."

4

IT'S A LIFELONG COMMITMENT

PRAYER

"Give me the strength to commit to this work for my lifetime."

The Pace of the kingdom

At the beginning of this book, I invited you to slow down.

I asked you not to rush and devour these pages in a weekend. I didn't want you to treat this as information to collect, but a process to experience.

That invitation wasn't just about how to read this book. It was how to live your life.

In our modern Western world, we're obsessed with instant results and early retirement. We're so conditioned to same-day deliveries, drive-thru dinner, and live-streaming entertainment, but the kingdom of God doesn't move at the pace of our culture.

It moves at the pace of eternity.

If you pay attention, creation itself reveals this rhythm. Seasons don't hurry. Tides rise and fall without anxiety. The moon completes its phases whether anyone is watching or not. Growth unfolds in layers, in cycles, in repetition.

The kingdom moves the same way.

Cathedrals stand as quiet witnesses to this truth. It's astonishing to consider how long it took to build those magnificent structures without modern machinery. Builders carved, lifted, and placed each stone by hand. They returned day after day, blistered and weary, committed to the work with no promise that they'd see it finished.

Many of them died before the final spire was lifted into place. Still, they showed up and laid stone upon stone. They trusted that faithfulness mattered more than speed.

The kingdom of God moves like that.

It's not rushed by technology or pressured by deadlines. It doesn't accelerate because you're anxious or slow down because you're afraid. It doesn't rearrange its rhythm because you beg it to accommodate you. Steady and sure, it continues to move, unfolding with a deeper wisdom.

When you say yes to building your cathedral, you're saying yes to that rhythm. You're committing to build at the pace of eternity.

Your yes is an agreement to keep showing up, to lay stones when no one notices, and to trust the process when you can't see the progress.

When you say yes, you're committing to a lifetime.

It's Going to Take a Lifetime

We've been conditioned to believe life is divided into phases of usefulness and irrelevance. You need to work hard, climb fast, and accumulate. Then retire at 65 and slowly fade into the background as if purpose has an expiration date, as if meaning diminishes with wrinkles, and usefulness declines with age.

But the kingdom of God doesn't retire its builders. The finish line is your last breath.

As long as you're breathing, you're meant to build. As long as your heart is beating, you're to expand. The kingdom never looks at a 70-year-old and says, "Your contribution is complete."

Look at nature closely, and you'll notice everything alive is growing.

An acorn doesn't grow for a few years and then declare itself finished. It spends its entire lifetime reaching deeper into the soil and higher into the sky. A mighty oak continues expanding its roots and widening its branches for as long as it lives.

Life and growth are inseparable. The moment growth stops, decay begins.

You were created with that same rhythm within you. Even though your body may slow and decline, your soul is meant to expand for as long as you have breath.

This is where faithful devotion to a lifelong commitment to building your cathedral becomes your greatest strength.

Faithfulness is choosing to grow slowly instead of quitting early. It's showing up when you can't see progress. It's trusting that the millimeters matter. It's believing that the foundation formed in hidden places will one day support something strong and enduring.

Michelangelo understood this kind of devotion. For four years, he lay suspended beneath the ceiling of the Sistine Chapel, painting inch by inch, with his muscles aching and his body strained. It wasn't glamorous work. It was daily, disciplined, painstaking work toward a vision.

In London, Westminster Abbey took five hundred years to complete. The builders who laid the first stones never saw the final arches. Generations worked to move the project forward, each one faithful to their part.

That is the pace of the kingdom.

The slow, steady work will take a long time—a lifetime.

Exhaustion Isn't God's kingdom

Hearing that there's no retirement in the kingdom of God may make you want to cry in your pillow from the dreadful thought. How could you work a lifetime building when you can barely make it through Tuesday without collapsing from exhaustion?

When you're striving, fatigue feels like a normal part of life. You live depleted and angry, hoping to get relief when you either retire or get to heaven.

But chronic burnout is not the rhythm of the kingdom. It's a sign that you're disconnected and in survival mode.

When you're in survival mode, you're pulling from a limited source. You're using your own strength, your own willpower, and your own anxious drive to achieve, obtain, or secure yourself. You're attempting to draw water from an empty well. Living like this leaves you resentful and depleted, and over time, you become a shell of yourself.

Building in God's will is different.

When you're in alignment, you live connected to the infinite source of Life. Like the oak tree pulls nutrients from the soil, water from rain, and rays of sunlight, you work with steady trust, receiving all that you need to build. You pace yourself, never panicked, never rushed. You no longer pull from your limited resources, but instead draw from a well that never runs dry.

That's not to say the work isn't hard. It is, and you may still feel tired at the end of a full day, but you're no longer hollow. You may face challenges, but they won't destroy you. You'll recover more quickly and return to your center more easily. You'll experience a strange paradox where you can work hard and still feel whole. You can give deeply, and your spirit still feels full.

Staying connected is how you build over a lifetime without burning out.

It's Never Too Late

When people begin to imagine what they want to build with their lives, shame often shows up first. They look back at the years behind them and immediately think, *It's too late for me.*

They convince themselves their best days are gone, that their window of opportunity has closed, or that everyone else is further along. They scroll through highlights of other people's successes and feel the weight of comparison pressing down on them. They feel like all they have to show for their life is crow's feet and a list of regrets.

This is a lie that you must immediately reject, because Jesus told a story about a man who hired men to do harvest work in his fields, some he hired early in the morning, some at noon, and even a few in the final hour. Yet when evening came, every worker received the same reward, not because of when they started, but because they said yes to the work.

That's the kingdom. It doesn't matter when you begin. If you start building in your youth or your final hour, you can still make something beautiful. You still have time. You're not too late or behind.

So whether you're eighteen or eighty, you're invited to begin with what's in your hands today, because once you glimpse what you're building, you'll never want to lay your hammer down.

Lift your eyes, and do not grow weary in your lifelong commitment to building your cathedral.

AFFIRMATION

"I'm building something beautiful that takes a lifetime."

YOUR COMMITMENT

I'm building a cathedral.
I'm building a life full of love and happiness for the
Divine to dwell.
The work is hard, mundane, and messy.
I commit to the work.
It's going to take a long time—a lifetime.
I commit to the time.
I commit to building a cathedral
and having fun doing it.

PART 2

A BUILDING PROJECT OF ONE—SUPPORTED BY THE ONE

EMPOWERMENT

5

THIS IS YOURS TO BUILD

PRAYER

"Thank You for entrusting me with my life. Give me the courage to build abundantly."

Learning to Drive

When I was sixteen, my dad decided I needed to learn how to drive a stick shift. He thought the best way was trial by fire. One evening, he drove me out to a hill on a back road in our small town, parked at the bottom, and said my goal was to drive his truck to the top.

There we sat, with me anxiously behind the wheel, and my dad calmly in the passenger seat. My knuckles were white on the steering wheel. My mind was spinning: *What if I crash? What if I can't do it?*

He told me to press the clutch with my left foot, the gas with my right, and to stay on the road. I released the clutch, hit the gas, and the truck lurched forward, sputtered, and died.

Over and over, I tried. I squealed the tires and killed the engine, but couldn't make it to the top. By the fifth or sixth attempt, as burning rubber filled the air, I began to cry.

I turned to my dad and begged, "Please, just do it for me." But he didn't.

He patiently said, "No. You're going to figure it out. It's going to be okay."

He was right. Eventually, I did figure it out. My dad's old truck somehow survived that night, and I finally made it up the hill. I figured it out, not because he took over, but because he didn't.

He knew it was my lesson to learn.

He Handed You the Tools to Build

When you were born, God handed you the tools for your life. For a while, your parents, teachers, and mentors helped you, but eventually, you were meant to pick up the hammer. And no matter how many times you mess up, cry, and beg God to, "Please take control," He won't.

He won't because He trusts you.

God gave you this life to build it, and He's not one to take His gifts back. He won't ever manipulate your work or override your free will. He sits there, calm and steady, guiding and encouraging you, pointing toward the blueprints and whispering directions. But in the end, the chisel is yours to hold.

Your life is divinely inspired, but humanly built. You're learning how to listen to the still small voice inside that guides you, but at the end of the day, you're the one who must grind the stones. You're the one who must learn to build walls and set the foundation. You're the one who must decide when it's time to stop, pivot, or keep going.

You're going to get it wrong sometimes. You'll hit rough patches, you'll grind too much, and you'll question if you're cut out for this. There's nothing to fear when you mess up. God isn't standing beside you with disappointment or judgment, waiting for you to get it perfect. Like a loving father who understands the limits of his child's strength, He has compassion for your humanity. He knows how you are formed, and he remembers that you are dust. He understands that you don't know what you don't know, that you're still learning how to build.

You're not meant to have it all figured out. You learn through experience. You lay a stone, see how it fits, and adjust. Even when you falter, He remains patient, trusting that, in time, you'll learn the divine rhythm and build the cathedral that once felt impossible.

Building Project of One

This is a building project of one. Out of billions of people on this earth, only you can build the cathedral of your life. No one else has your exact desires, gifts, or experiences. God entrusted this work to you alone.

Even if you're married, raising children, or part of a community, your construction is still yours. Your spouse's choices, your children's paths, or your friends' opinions don't determine the work you were asked to build. They can love and support you, but you cannot hand your tools over to them. They have their own cathedrals to build.

This isn't isolation, but ownership. It's understanding that what God placed in you is sacred and nontransferable. You're responsible for showing up to work with your own hands and heart. Mentors or loved ones may support you along the way, but the work belongs to you and God alone.

When you grasp that truth, comparison loses its grip. You stop measuring your pace against anyone else's because you realize you're not building the same cathedral. Every person's project is different. Some grand, some small, some seen, some hidden, but all are holy.

Your Cathedral to Build

This cathedral, your life, is yours to build. God provides the guidance and the materials, but He entrusts you with the work.

He won't build it for you, but He will build with you.

You may not always know the plan. You may not understand the timing or the terrain, but you can trust that the same Spirit who breathed life into you will guide your hands as you shape your life.

Pick up your tools, for this is yours to build.

AFFIRMATION

"My cathedral is divinely inspired, but humanly built."

6

THE BLESSING OF WORK

PRAYER

"Let my work, no matter how small, be a reflection of You."

Your Privilege to Work

Everything changed for Adam and Eve after they ate from the tree of the knowledge of good and evil. Standing at the edge of the garden, dressed in suede, they listened as God established the new order by which humanity would live.

From that day forward, He declared man would bring forth fruit by the sweat of his brow.

It's easy to see that moment as punishment, as though Adam was cursed, but it wasn't Adam who was cursed. It was the ground.

If you look closer at God's new order, you'll see it wasn't a curse, but a transfer of creative power. Up until that moment,

God had created everything, and Adam and Eve lounged in his handiwork.

God would no longer be the only one creating. Humanity now played an active role in the creation process. The work bestowed upon man was divine power flowing through human hands. It was God saying, *Now you will build with Me.*

That moment established the universal law of sowing and reaping, giving and receiving. Like gravity, it's a law that can't be broken. You can ignore it, deny it, or resist it, but you can't escape it. We are bound to this law.

From that day forward, humanity stepped into responsibility. Good or evil, what you plant will eventually grow. What you give, you will receive.

It was the first labor law written: you reap what you sow.

When you miss the gift that comes with work, you'll see it as the enemy. You'll attempt to avoid it, thinking peace and happiness come from escaping it. You'll look for ways to do less and rush through, enduring until you can finally retire and be free.

But life's fulfillment isn't outside the work you do, it's within it.

The Blessing of Work

When you work in alignment with the creative power that God bestowed on man instead of against it, you discover that meaning comes from the work itself. The joy of reaping is the reward of the effort of sowing. There is no satisfaction without participating in creative work.

A store-bought cookie might satisfy your craving, but it's

far more fulfilling to sink your teeth into a warm, gooey cookie that your hands made. Not only are they more satisfying to eat, but you also feel more compelled to share your yummy creation with others.

Work does more than produce results. It produces meaning, fulfillment, and divine connection.

The hidden blessing of work is that it invites you into the flow of creation. You move from being a spectator of life to a contributor to it. You don't wake each day only consuming what exists. You actively co-create what will exist next.

Our culture glorifies the four-hour work week and romanticizes passive income, as if the ultimate achievement were leisure. We measure success by how far we can distance ourselves from responsibility. But in doing so, we rob ourselves of a sacred partnership.

When you work in alignment, labor becomes the channel through which you find meaning. Whether you're teaching a child, repairing a faucet, managing a team, or sweeping a floor, you're in partnership with the Divine.

With purpose, you live with expectancy. Each day holds possibilities because you know you're contributing to something larger. You're making a difference. There's a deep thrill in knowing you're building a cathedral.

If your current work feels unfulfilling, don't despise it. Practice gratitude for the opportunity to earn, to create, and to develop in discipline and skill. Hold a vision for more meaningful work if your heart longs for it, but don't abandon integrity in your present work.

Labor faithfully by the sweat of your brow, because in time you'll reap your harvest.

The Sacred Exchange

Within your labor, there's a sacred exchange that occurs. As you give yourself to your work, your work gives back fulfillment, meaning, and joy.

You're participating in the sacred exchange of giving and receiving.

Kahlil Gibran captured this truth when he wrote, "To love life through labor is to be intimate with life's inmost secret."

The secret is when you pour yourself into your work, God pours Himself back into you.

Think of a kindergartener holding up her glitter-covered construction paper. She can hardly wait to show you what she made. Her eyes light up as she explains every detail, proud of every crooked line and clump of glue.

Her joy doesn't come from the project's perfection. She isn't wondering if it's good enough or whether she's worthy of creating it.

Her joy comes from her participation in creation. She made something that didn't exist before.

In that moment, something deeper is happening. The creative spark moving through her is the same divine spark that brought the universe into being. As she pours herself into her little masterpiece, the Creator is quietly expressing Himself through her.

The sacred exchange isn't reserved for children. It's alive in the accountant balancing numbers, the nurse tending wounds, the mother making breakfast, and the truck driver delivering materials that will become someone's home.

We can witness the natural sacred exchange in little children, but we were never meant to outgrow that spark.

Your Work Doesn't Define You

Somewhere along the way, many of us forgot it.

Instead of experiencing work as a sacred exchange, we begin using it as a measuring stick for our worth.

When that happens, work quietly shifts from an act of creation to an act of proving. If you carry a hidden belief that you aren't enough, worthy, or capable, work becomes the place you try to close that gap.

You begin striving for outcomes instead of participating in the process. You push yourself to work harder, achieve more, and chase results, hoping that the next accomplishment will finally prove you're enough.

When your identity becomes tied to the outcome of your work, satisfaction is always just out of reach. Even when you achieve something meaningful, the feeling doesn't last long. There's always another milestone to reach, another achievement to secure, and another validation to chase. Your sense of self goes up and down with every review, paycheck, compliment, or criticism.

You can recognize if your identity is linked to your work by how personal it is to you. Does criticism of your work feel like criticism of you? Does your self-esteem fluctuate with your successes and mistakes? Do you feel threatened when things don't go as planned?

This kind of striving is exhausting because it's built on the wrong foundation. Your work isn't a test to prove your worth. It's meant to be an expression of it.

That little girl didn't become enough because she created something of value. She expressed her worth by participating in the creative process.

Before you ever lifted a hand, spoke a word, or accomplished a skill, you were already worthy, loved, and approved. Your value has nothing to do with what you accomplish and everything to do with your essence being in the image of God.

As you learn to align yourself in Love and begin to operate from the Divine abundance, your work will become an expression of your worth. Work will stop being a performance and become participation. Every task, big or small, becomes an offering of gratitude rather than a desperate attempt at validation.

Whatever work is in front of you today, whether it's emails, spreadsheets, dishes, lesson plans, repairs, or pouring concrete, do it in Love. Do it with integrity. Do it with the awareness that something unseen is happening within you and through you as you work.

You're participating in a sacred exchange, and in that exchange, there is more than a paycheck or a résumé.

There's a cathedral.

AFFIRMATION

"My work is sacred. I co-create with the Divine in every task I do."

7

THE HUMAN PARADOX

PRAYER

"When I tremble on the edge of fear, remind me that You keep me safe."

You're Powerful and Vulnerable

Deep within, you sense your capacity for greatness. You have the potential to dream, create, build, transform, and change the direction of your life. We still don't know the limits of human potential. You've seen glimpses of this greatness in yourself, and you've watched it manifest in others. You're very powerful.

Yet, in the same breath, you know how fragile this life is. Your body can break. Your heart can be shattered. One diagnosis, one accident, one phone call can end everything. You make mistakes, stumble, and fall. You're very vulnerable.

In each human, there's great power and great vulnerability. You're more capable than you realize, but you're far more fragile than you'd like to admit.

Both are true at the same time.

This is what I call the Human Paradox.

You're equal parts powerful and vulnerable, infinite and finite. You have a divine knowing and human unknowing all at once.

You're walking dust, holding the Eternal.

It's a tightrope learning to live securely in the tension between these extremes.

Most people never reach their true potential because their fear of their vulnerabilities paralyzes them. They choose to bury their greatness to protect themselves from their weaknesses.

When the mountaintops call them higher, and they feel the pull of greatness, they long to climb, but fear of failing keeps them small. The height shows both what's possible and what could be lost.

The wind whispers, "Come away with me."

But fear warns, "You could fall."

Caught between potential and fear, they retreat to safety, convincing themselves that the ground below is enough. They decide to bury their talent to keep it safe, even as something inside them aches for more.

Let Go and Trust

A few years ago, I joined a group for an outdoor team-building course high up in the trees. There were ropes, ladders, and catwalks suspended in the air.

When my turn came to climb up, fear flooded my body. I

didn't think I was afraid of heights, but even after the guide clipped me into a safety harness, my legs trembled.

Halfway across the rope net, I froze, unable to move forward or back. My arms and legs were shaking uncontrollably as I did my best to hold on to the ropes.

The instructor called out, "Don't hold on so tight! Let go and trust your safety harness!"

He sounded insane. *Let go?* My death grip was the only thing keeping me from falling!

As my shaking arms gave out, I was forced to loosen my grip and lean back. To my shock, the harness actually caught me.

I was safe.

I knew I was more than capable of completing the course, but my awareness of my vulnerability paralyzed me from finishing. I wanted to move forward, but the fear of falling kept me frozen. I tried to control my fear by holding on to the ropes tighter. It gave me the illusion of safety while keeping me stuck in one place. The more I tried to manage my anxiety, the more power it gained over me.

We cling to invisible ropes of fear, terrified of losing control, afraid of failing, of being alone, of not having enough. We pray for peace but hold onto our anxiety like a lifeline.

The truth is, you already have a safety rope. Every one of us is clipped into the unbreakable cord of Love. You don't have to earn it. You don't have to prove yourself worthy of it. It comes standard issue at birth.

When you finally loosen your grip and trust the rope, you realize it's been holding you all along.

That rope of Love keeps you steady as you climb the scaffolding of your cathedral. The scaffolding may shake, the wind may howl, and the heights may terrify you, but the rope is secure. You're safe to build and rise.

Trust is believing that the safety rope is holding you, so you can let go and build something great.

But here's what makes things complicated. Even if the rope is secure, even if Love is holding you, if you don't believe it, it doesn't matter. You'll still feel insecure. You still won't feel safe. When fear wins, fear controls.

Two Dogs Inside You

There's an old story of a wise elder who said, "Inside me are two dogs. One is fear, and the other is love. They fight all the time."

"Which one wins?" the boy asked.

"The one I feed the most," he replied.

Trust is the food that feeds the dogs. Fear breeds anxiety and exhaustion. Love breeds peace and abundance.

Where you place your trust determines which one rules inside you. When you dwell on your fears, you're trusting the lies that fear tells you, and that dog grows stronger, but when you turn toward Love and feed it with your trust, that dog grows stronger.

You're the keeper of both dogs. You decide which one you'll feed, which one will win.

Next time fear grips you, pause, and feed Love.

One thing you can do is lie down on the earth or your bed. Close your eyes. Breathe deeply. Feel the ground holding you. Hear the whisper of the Divine saying, *Relax. You're safe. You don't have to do anything. I got you.*

If the earth can hold you, if gravity can keep you anchored, how much more can Love hold you as you build your cathedral?

You're safe.

Your children are safe.

Your future is safe.

You can trust Him.

Trust the Rope of Love

Even in uncertainty, you're being held. The rope of the Divine is what makes it possible to live in the tension of power and vulnerability.

You don't need to cling so tightly by trying to manage every outcome and to control every circumstance. Lean back into the rope. Let Love hold you. That's what He's there for.

As you stand between your great potential and your human limitation, ask Him, "Can I trust You with what I cannot control, with my family, my future, and my life?"

Then listen until you hear the still, small voice that answers, "Yes, I got you."

AFFIRMATION

"I release my grip on fear and lean into the rope of Love."

8

THIS CATHEDRAL ISN'T YOURS

PRAYER

"Teach me to with open hands and a humble heart."

You're a Tenant, Not the Owner

You'll spend your life laying one stone after another with devotion and care. You'll build your cathedral with intention. You'll pour your vision, your labor, and your passion into its walls.

But this cathedral isn't yours. You don't hold the deed, and you aren't the owner. You're a tenant on borrowed land.

You didn't earn this life. You were born into a story already unfolding. Long before you arrived, others labored, sacrificed, and built. Their faith paved the road that you now walk on.

Every breath you take is a loan. Every opportunity is the continuation of someone else's work.

When Jesus told the story of the servants entrusted with talents, the master didn't give them ownership of the talents. He gave them stewardship. They never owned the treasure. They only managed it.

That's your life.

The time you've been given is sacred capital on loan. The gifts in your hands are entrusted, not owned. Some people are given five talents, some two, some one. Some begin in abundance; others, in poverty. The starting point is never equal.

But the measure of your life isn't determined by what you start with. It's determined by what you do with what's been loaned to you.

The one who multiplies a small gift is just as faithful as the one who begins with much.

Society teaches that your value is found in ownership. We say things like 'my house,' 'my career,' and 'my accomplishments.' But everything you call mine is temporary. Your home will shelter another family. Your work will be continued by someone else. Your possessions will pass into other hands.

You're a tenant in this body and on this earth. Ownership is an illusion.

The cathedral of your life isn't a monument to you. It's a conduit between heaven and earth.

When you begin to cling to physical things, calling them mine with tight fists, you cut yourself off from the Divine flow. Anxiety increases as your fear of losing them grows, and the more you fear losing, the more you attempt to control them. That's when you become a slave to your possessions.

Be careful not to attach yourself to things. They're not yours to possess or to own. All that you see, taste, and touch is owned by a much higher power. They are His to give and His to take away. They aren't your source of safety, power, or wealth. Steward them with open hands.

Your Gift of Gratitude

The cathedral you build is your gift of gratitude to God, to those who came before you, and to those who will follow you.

But before we talk about your gift of gratitude, we need to understand what gratitude truly is.

Most of us think gratitude means being thankful *for* something, usually something we find pleasant, like a promotion, a healing, or a opened door. We give thanks when life feels kind.

But we're asked to give thanks in all things.

How do you give thanks for the painful experiences like loss, betrayal, or illness?

You do this by detaching your gratitude from things and experiences, and practicing gratitude that isn't attached to circumstances or dependent on outcomes.

True gratitude is an emotional response to the awareness that no matter what happens around you, good or bad, you're always connected to the infinite source of Life. It's the quiet confidence that provision will always come, that Love will never withdraw, and you're continually sustained.

It isn't rooted in what you receive, but in who you're connected to.

When gratitude is anchored in Love, it becomes unshakable. It can coexist with tears. It can stand in the rubble. It can whisper thank You even when you still don't understand.

It's from that kind of gratitude that you build.

You build first for God, whose Spirit stirs within you the desire to create. When you fold laundry with patience, speak kindly when it's hard, or work with excellence, these become sacred acts of gratitude. The work itself is worship. Your steady hands and faithful heart are offerings to the One who imagined you into being.

You also build in gratitude for those who came before you. The infinite Spirit supported your ancestors, mentors, and unknown laborers as they made sacrifices to make your foundation possible. They cleared the ground, carried the burdens, and laid the stones that gave you something to build upon. Every time your hammer strikes, you're working in humble devotion to their contribution.

Finally, you build for those who will come after you. For the ones who will walk these halls and find shelter beneath the arches you raise. They may never know your name, but they'll feel your spirit in the strength of the walls and the beauty that surrounds them. You build so they can stand taller and live fuller.

You're not building for applause or validation. You're building as a conduit between heaven and earth, past and future, Creator and creation.

Every brick you lay is a prayer of gratitude.

You're Building Something Greater Than You

This cathedral isn't yours, and it never was, but you're blessed beyond measure to be part of its creation.

You're a builder in a story far larger than yourself. You're a servant of eternity.

Your life is a prayer, your work an offering, and your breath a thank-you.

So take up your tools again. Wipe the dust from your hands and feel the weight of what has been entrusted to you.

This is holy work.

Lay each stone as if heaven itself were watching, because it is.

Let every effort be an act of Love. Don't rush or demand that it unfold in your way or in your time. Trust the process of something greater.

Your hands may never see its completion, but your fingerprints will remain on its walls. What you build today will outlast you. Long after your name is forgotten, your spirit will still echo through the halls of what you created.

When your season of building is done, when your body grows tired, and the tools slip from your hands, you'll see what Love built through you.

Then, bless the one who picks up your chisel:

I've built my part. Now you must build yours.
Let your work rise higher, and your reach expand
further.
May your stones stand with hope,
and your cathedral shine with Love.

AFFIRMATION

"I am building with a heart of gratitude."

PART 3

WRITING A BLUEPRINT

VISION

9

WITHOUT A VISION,
YOU WILL PERISH

PRAYER

"Open my inner eyes to see the vision of my cathedral. Awaken the dream buried beneath distraction and fear."

Transformation of Saint-Denis Abbey

As a young boy, Abbot Suger's family sent him to the old, crumbling abbey of Saint-Denis on the outskirts of Paris to begin his training as a monk. Most of the abbey's residents despised the dark, decaying building, but Suger fell in love with it and longed to rebuild it.

As the years passed, Suger's unshakable vision of the abbey being restored never faded. After becoming abbot, the time finally came for him to lead its reconstruction. He poured his whole being into the work, pioneering the movement that ushered in the Gothic architectural era.

The only reason Saint-Denis Abbey was transformed was

because of Abbot Suger's vision. Before builders laid the first stone, the cathedral already existed in his imagination. That's the power of vision. It gives form to what does not yet exist.

Vision is the inner architecture of creation. It's first creating a picture in your mind, and then believing it with your whole heart. Without a vision, the builders have no direction, and nothing is ever accomplished. But when a person holds a vision with clarity and faith, in time, the empty field will become a sanctuary.

Abbot Suger saw light where others saw decay. He saw beauty where others saw rubble. Vision gives you eyes to see beyond your current circumstances. It lifts your focus from present reality to future possibility. And when you hold that vision long enough, it begins to take shape in your material world.

Without It, You'll Perish

Vision isn't optional.

It's not a luxury for dreamers or entrepreneurs, and it's not only reserved for the ambitious. It's vital to the success, happiness, and fulfillment of your life.

I would go so far as to say it's impossible to live your life without it, because where there is no vision, the people perish. It's not that you'll only waste away spiritually, but also emotionally, physically, and directionally. You'll lose vibrance, clarity, and eventually you'll lose yourself.

Matt and I are in the middle of building a house. For months, we reviewed hundreds of blueprints, debated layouts, measured spaces, and revised plans. We hashed out every detail, considering where the light would fall, what rooms we wanted and needed, and how the spaces would function.

All before one shovel touched the ground.

Because without clarity, we couldn't build a house. We have to capture the vision of what we're building before we can make it happen in reality.

If we walked onto our land and told the builder, "Build us a house. We'll check back in six months."

We'd come back to find a disaster if there were even a house to inspect at all.

Your life is no different.

If you wake up each day without vision, simply reacting to what's in front of you, you may be busy, but you won't be building. You may be moving, but you won't be moving toward anything.

Vision gives direction to your work. It ensures that the stones you lay today actually belong to the structure you hope to see tomorrow.

Vision is Your Blueprint

Once you have a vision, it becomes your blueprint. It becomes your internal guide when the work in front of you feels uncertain. A vision doesn't tell you how to build, but points you toward your end. It's the orientation of your soul that keeps you aligned when distractions or detours try to pull you off course.

Vision anchors you. It keeps you moving forward when progress is slow, when doors close, or when the next step isn't clear. It reminds you why you started and what you're building toward. Without direction, you wander, but with vision, you live with intention.

I know I'm talking in high-level life visions, but this principle applies to the simplest things. It's your vision of having a clean house that gets you off the couch to begin the mundane housework. Your vision is what keeps you scrubbing toilets and mopping floors.

Vision turns repetition into devotion. It breathes life into your labor.

When your vision becomes your blueprint, you no longer depend on constant external validation. You stop chasing approval, and criticism loses its power to derail you. You know where you're headed because the direction lives within you.

Vision doesn't remove uncertainty, but it gives meaning to the journey, and that meaning is what keeps you faithfully building.

Vision Gives Your Work Meaning

In the tale of two masons, both men worked the same job. Both chiseled, sweated, and shaped stones. One labored in frustration, while the other worked toward his greater vision. The first mason only saw the rock in front of him, but the second mason could see what the rock would become.

When you have a greater vision, your work has meaning. The daily routine becomes bearable because you're anchored to a vision of what's coming.

Many people live aimlessly. They get up, work, scroll, sleep, and repeat. And if you ask them why they do it, they'll shrug and say, "It's just life. It's what you do."

But that's not living. That's existing.

When you wander through life, you'll eventually end up in the back alleys of debt, broken relationships, and quiet despair.

Existing is stacking stones, but building nothing.

Remember Your Vision

Abbot Suger's dream of Saint-Denis didn't become a cathedral because he imagined it. It became a cathedral because he envisioned its completion and remained faithful to that vision over the years until it became a physical reality.

It's not enough to glimpse the beauty of what could be and forget about it. You must keep that image alive through every season of building, trusting that what began as inspiration will one day take form. You must remember your vision.

Don't let another day pass without a vision guiding your hands.

Dare to dream again, and commit to seeing what others cannot, and then hold that vision in your mind as you build it, one faithful day at a time.

Your vision is ready.

Pick up your pen, and begin.

AFFIRMATION

"I'm creating a vision for my life, imagining it in its fullness."

10

ENVISION THE END

PRAYER

"Support me as I create my living cathedral through the power of my imagination."

Power of Your Imagination

To create a vision, you must first see beyond your current reality and, in your mind, construct a new possibility that doesn't yet exist. Imagination is the place where the formless comes into being. In your mind, you can literally create something from nothing. Your capacity to do this is what sets you apart from all other living creatures. This power is what it means to be made in God's image.

God looked upon formless void and spoke creation into existence, but before he could speak it, he had to see it.

The psalmist confirms this with, "Your eyes saw my unformed body."

Before he formed, he imagined.

When you imagine, you're not escaping reality. You're participating in the same creative energy that began it all. Your imagination is a holy participation in the creative flow.

But many people have neglected their imagination.

As children, we used it freely by turning cardboard boxes into forts and sticks into swords. We lived with constant wonder, seeing endless possibilities, but somewhere along the way, we traded imagination for practicality. We stopped dreaming and started surviving.

Over time, your divine spark dimmed, leaving you to wander in darkness, feeling so lost and alone. You didn't do anything wrong. You forgot your power. You weren't meant to live disconnected from the creative flow.

Your imagination isn't just a childhood fantasy, but a mighty, powerful force that you must revive. You must ignite the spark and find your light again.

Reviving Your Imagination

If you've spent years surviving, it can feel awkward, even foolish, to imagine again. Remember, you're not a silly child playing make-believe. You're learning how to reawaken your creative power to multiply your life. Your discomfort is because your imagination muscle hasn't moved in a while. The more you practice, the stronger it becomes.

Start small. You don't need to go straight for the big life vision. Instead, dream about a corner of your home that you can decorate for reading and praying. Picture how your kitchen will look and feel cleaned and organized. Imagine yourself all dressed up, eating a special dinner with someone you love.

Use the world around you as your inspiration. Clip magazine images, start a vision board, or read books that stir up possibilities. Put yourself in the picture, imagine you're living in the house, driving the car, or cooking the delicious meals. Write down your visions so you don't forget them.

Vision is What, Not How or When

Often, as soon as we allow ourselves to imagine something beautiful or expansive about life, our logical mind steps in and shuts it down.

There's no way this will ever happen. Have you seen your life?

You really think you could afford that?

How in the world do you plan to make that happen?

We have a habit of stuffing our God-given gift in a back closet when we can't see when or how our vision could ever come true.

Please don't get hung up on the how or when. That part is above your pay grade. Leave that up to God to orchestrate. Your part is the what (vision) and the why (purpose).

Your job is to hold your vision in mind, stay faithful to the work in front of you, and trust that God will figure out the rest.

Give yourself all the creative freedom to practice expanding your thoughts in Love with no expectation of whether they're right or wrong, if they will or won't happen. Enjoy it like a child. This is your time to have fun with God, thinking of all the things you could create together. Keep going, you're learning how to dream again.

As you practice creating small visions, something will shift. The fog will start to lift, and larger dreams will begin to emerge.

Envision the End (The 80 Test)

Coming up with a life vision can be overwhelming and intimidating, so when you're ready to tackle it, I created an exercise that will help you uncover what your soul truly desires.

To capture a vision for your life, start at the end. Go to your final chapter of life story and imagine what you built. I call it The 80 Test.

Sit somewhere quiet and close your eyes. Take a deep breath and picture yourself at eighty years old, sitting peacefully at your kitchen table. Your hands are weathered and a bit shaky as you hold a warm cup of your favorite drink. The room hums with life. Family and friends surround you, and the air is full of laughter.

What do you see in your home? Where do you live? Who is surrounding you?

What have you contributed to your community, your family, and the world? How do you feel about the life you've built?

Take as much time as you need to allow your imagination to run free. Now, write down everything that comes to mind as a stream of consciousness, meaning you write without filtering your thoughts. Don't stop yourself with logic. Just write, allowing your soul to speak.

Every time you envision the end, your cathedral takes shape. You may not know exactly how it will all come together, but the vision gives something to work toward.

Surrender Your Vision

Many struggle with vision because they fear getting it wrong, worry that their desires aren't holy, or feel selfish for wanting those beautiful things.

In Chapter Two, we discussed how you can align your vision with God's divine will by asking yourself one simple question: "Is this rooted in Love?"

If your vision flows from Love for God, for others, and for the world, then you are already aligned with his will. Love never leads to greed or pride. It always leads to creation, healing, and growth.

Once you're sure your vision is rooted in Love, it's time to release it. Even though you imagined it with your creative power and you aligned it with Love, it still isn't yours to worry about, strive towards, or chase after. It's yours to offer it back to God with open hands, so he can begin his good work of orchestrating his part — the how and the when.

You give it back to him with a prayer, "This, or something better."

That simple phrase keeps your spirit aligned with God's higher path, releasing it from having to go your way and in your time. It's an acknowledgment that, while your vision matters, God sees the bigger picture, including details you can't yet perceive.

For example, let's say you envision a beautiful home with warm, sunlit rooms, high ceilings, a cozy kitchen, and a big yard where you can watch your kids play. You picture every detail, including the color of the walls, the way the light filters through the windows, and even the feeling of peace you have as you sip your morning coffee. You see Love in every detail of your vision, so you start planning for that dream home.

But then, things don't go quite as you expected. The market shifts, the house you wanted sells to someone else, or life redirects you. At first, disappointment sets in because you think you've missed what was meant to be. Many times this is where people abandon their vision, interpreting the shift as not being God's will after all.

Yet in time, another door opens. You find a different home you would've never considered before in a different neighborhood with a different layout. Still, when you walk through the door, you realize it's everything you actually wanted and needed. It fits your lifestyle, your finances, and your peace in ways you couldn't have imagined.

That's the power of saying, "This, or something better."

It's an act of surrendering your limitations to a higher Source without limitations. You're making room for divine wisdom to refine your vision, and for God to exceed your expectations.

What you imagine is the starting point. Give it room to evolve.

Build with Open Hands

Hold your vision in your mind, but work with open hands. This isn't your cathedral to grip with white knuckles. Part of the co-creative process is learning to trust that your greatest gifts are always on their way, not necessarily exactly as you pictured, but in the form that's perfectly designed for you.

Keep your hands open, because you can't see the whole path. You don't fully know the depths of your own heart. What you think you want today may only be a glimpse of a much greater desire waiting to be revealed. When you release your attachment to how it must look, you give God room to surprise you with something exceedingly abundantly above all that you ask or think.

Think of your vision as a living organism, always growing and evolving as you do.

Don't be afraid to dream, envision, and take action, but remember to keep your hands open. Release your fear that you're being selfish or getting it wrong. Keep saying yes to the stirring within you, and the Divine will handle the rest.

You imagine. God directs.

You envision. God orchestrates.

You build. God supports.

Together, you co-create the cathedral of your life.

AFFIRMATION

"I hold my vision in my mind and work with open hands."

11

BELIEVE IT BEFORE YOU SEE IT

PRAYER

"Strengthen me as I learn to trust and believe in what I cannot see."

***

Without Faith, It's Impossible to Build

Without faith, it's impossible to build a cathedral. It's impossible to build a healthy marriage, a fulfilling career, or an abundant life without it. Faith is the bridge between the unseen and the seen, between the vision in your mind and the reality in your hands.

The word faith has been used so often that it's become a Christian cliché. It sounds good when we say it, yet few people can clearly explain what it actually means.

We hear phrases like, 'You need to have faith.' Or 'Have faith in God.' Or 'Faith over fear.' They sound inspiring, but what does 'have faith' really mean?

Stripped of religious jargon and spiritual clichés, faith means you believe your unseen vision is true before you have any visible proof.

When a cathedral is built, it begins with a vision of arches, stained glass, and soaring spires. At first, it's invisible, just an idea in the architect's mind and lines on paper, but the builders begin anyway. They dig, pour, and chip, as if the cathedral already exists, because in their minds, it does.

Faith is evidence that what you cannot see is already real.

It's easy to believe in what you can see. Anyone can trust a finished building, a full bank account, or a thriving marriage. But faith asks something deeper: *Will you believe before there's proof? Will you act as if it's already done, even when there's no visible sign of progress?*

Faith is Believing Before Seeing

Now that we have defined faith as believing before seeing, the next question that never gets answered is: What does believing actually look like?

Belief isn't wishful thinking. Belief is trust, but if you're unclear about what you're trusting, it can feel like crossing your fingers and hoping for the best. People will usually say they believe in God or trust God, but again, what does trusting God mean? What does that look like on a Tuesday afternoon?

In Chapter Six, we covered how God introduced the natural law of sowing and reaping, or giving and receiving, in the story of Adam and Eve. This is one of God's laws that defines His divine order. It's in these unbreakable and unchanging laws that you put your trust.

For instance, if you have a watermelon seed, knowing the law, you trust that once planted, even though it's hidden, it's not dead. You know that beneath the surface, forces are at work.

In time, the watermelon in your mind will be a watermelon in your hand. The vision is already established. Nature is just working to make it happen in the material world.

Faith isn't denying what you see. It's not ignoring the fact that nothing has sprouted yet. You're not pretending you're looking at a watermelon in front of you. Faith acknowledges the present circumstances, but it also trusts a deeper reality at work in the unseen realm.

You understand that growth follows order. You must put in effort before the harvest, and roots form before fruit appears.

You don't panic when the seed is buried. You don't dig it up every day to check on it. You trust that what you plant will reap a harvest in its proper time.

Faith is having confidence in the unseen order. It's resting in the understanding that there is structure behind life. The sun will rise. The seasons will change. Seeds will grow. Cause will produce effect.

When you believe, you're not denying reality. You're aligning yourself with a higher one.

Faith Always Acts

Imagine your spouse says, "I'm going to buy you a new couch."

Let's break down how faith works in the simplest terms.

First comes vision.

You look past your worn cushions and imagine a new cozy couch. You go to Pinterest or your friend's living room for inspiration, and with time, you lock in on an inner vision of the couch you desire. Now, that vision becomes your blueprint, your end goal.

Next comes your faith.

It's not enough to just imagine the couch and forget about it. You must believe a new couch is possible. You trust that it's already on its way, not by wiggling your nose and waiting for it to spawn in your living room, but by aligning yourself with the higher spiritual law.

You know that if you plant, you will reap. If you give, you will receive.

You're not putting your trust in your husband, your money, or in magic. You're putting your faith in the higher law at work.

Then comes action.

Faith always acts, because co-creation requires participation.

If you trust your couch is on the way, you'll prepare for it. You'll set money aside, sell the old couch, and measure the space. Even though the new one hasn't arrived, your behavior shows confidence that it will.

You know the right couch will present itself at the right time, in the right way, and for the right price.

Now, consider the opposite.

Let's say you're unaware of the law, so you believe a new couch isn't possible. You trust that it's not coming because you can't afford it or something will fall through. You don't save or scroll Pinterest or sell your couch.

Instead, you shrug and say, "I'll believe it when I see it," and settle back on the old cushions.

Both are acting according to their faith. One believes it's possible and prepares. One believes it isn't possible and does nothing.

Action always reveals your belief.

Faith without works is dead, because it's through action that you participate in the co-creation.

Faith Feels Risky

Living by faith is one of the hardest things you'll ever do, because it asks you to act before you see results. It requires you to move forward when your current circumstances don't yet reflect what you're building toward.

There's always a gap between vision and evidence, and that gap is where fear lives.

It's normal to feel doubt when the bank account is empty or feel anxiety when the marriage is struggling. It's normal to feel exposed when you lose a job.

In Chapter Seven, *The Human Paradox*, we explored how you're both powerful and vulnerable at the same time. You carry greatness, strength, and incredible capacity, and yet you're limited, fragile, and deeply aware of how quickly life can change.

It can feel impossible to trust when you're so vulnerable, and it's in that vulnerability that fear takes root.

Fear whispers, *You're not safe. If this doesn't work out, you'll lose. If you step out and fall, you'll never recover. If things go wrong, you'll be alone.*

Underneath your fear is a deeper question: Am I safe in my vulnerability?

Faith goes beyond just trusting in the law of sowing and reaping. It's trust in the foundational truth that you are held, that God isn't working against you, but for you. It's trusting that the painful, delayed, or unwanted experiences are all working for your good.

We tend to judge experiences as good or bad based on whether we like them. If it feels pleasant, we call it a blessing. If it hurts, we call it failure. But faith dares to believe that discomfort isn't the same as danger, and limitations aren't the same as abandonment.

Fear says, *If this doesn't go my way, I won't be okay.*

Faith says, *Even if this doesn't go my way, I'm still held.*

As you continue building, your faith will strengthen as the divine Spirit confirms again and again that he is in all and through all, working for your good.

Your fear doesn't mean you don't have faith. It means you're a human learning to walk by faith. You'll be shaky, weak, and trembling, but whatever you do, don't stop walking.

Keep building.

Action Activates the Invisible

Faith always acts, and it's through action that you activate the invisible.

Consider the watermelon seed again. If you want fruit, you don't leave the seed on the kitchen counter and stare at it, hoping it appears. That isn't faith. That's fantasy.

Faith understands order.

You place the seed in the soil. Then, you water it, pull weeds, and protect the vine from pests. You do your part.

But you can't force it to grow.

You don't command the cells to divide or stretch the vine toward the sun. Life is already embedded within the seed by God Himself. Growth is written into creation.

Your action doesn't create life. It activates it.

Paul said, "I planted, Apollos watered, but God gave the increase."

When you plant, you align yourself with the law of sowing and reaping. When you tend the soil, you cooperate with the unseen processes already at work. You plant. God gives the growth.

Now consider something less biological, like the couch.

There's no seed with life inside it. There isn't a natural growth cycle in the couch, yet the same principle applies.

If you believe a new couch is possible, you prepare by saving money and clearing the space. You also begin paying attention.

That's when something shifts. Maybe a friend casually mentions she's selling her couch. Maybe you notice a sale you would have previously ignored. Maybe one appears at the right time and within your budget.

Your preparation doesn't force the outcome. It positions you for it.

The Spirit is always moving, and provision is always flowing, but you only step into what you're prepared to receive.

What some call coincidence, faith calls providence.

Your faith doesn't bend heaven to your will. It's you

aligning your will with heaven's order. It's trusting that when you move in accordance with what you believe, unseen forces are already working alongside you.

You act. God opens.

What once existed only in your imagination begins to take form in your hands.

Build by Faith, Not Sight

Building by faith is the narrow way that few find because it asks more of you than almost anything else. It asks you to trust when you can't see, to move when you're unsure, and to keep laying stones when nothing makes sense.

Faith will stretch you. It will humble you, expose your fears, and test your resolve.

Yet, without faith, it's impossible to build.

Every cathedral began as a vision no one else could see. Every restored marriage, every healed heart, and every meaningful life was built by someone who chose to believe before there was proof.

This is difficult work. Be patient with yourself. You're learning to walk by faith. You're learning to trust the unseen order and build in partnership with an unseen God. This is sacred work.

Fear will never entirely disappear. In fact, it'll be your companion for a long time, but it won't control you forever.

As the Spirit responds to your faith, confirming that He can be trusted, your confidence will grow. Over time, the work will get easier, and the weight will feel lighter.

One day, you'll realize the unseen that once terrified you became the very cathedral in front of you.

Keep building. By faith.

AFFIRMATION

"I build by faith, not by sight. What is unseen within me is more real than what I see around me."

12

PREPARING TO BUILD

PRAYER

"Give me courage to stand still on my holy ground and clear the land."

Surveying the Land

When Matt and I bought our land in the country to begin building our dream home, I imagined we'd close on the property, roll up our sleeves, and start building right away. But we quickly learned it doesn't work that way.

Before a shovel broke ground, we had to survey the land. We ordered soil tests to determine where it was safe to build and water tests to confirm we could dig a well. We spent weeks brush-hogging overgrown pastures and cutting back wild underbrush that had taken over.

What looked like a perfect property at first turned out to

be riddled with soft spots, low areas prone to flooding, and tangled barbed-wire fences.

That's how life works, too. Before you start writing goals or chasing dreams, you must take an honest look at your current life. Before you build anything new, you must walk the land of your life with reverence. Survey every corner. Notice the broken walls, the overgrown weeds, and the neglected spaces.

You can't start an investment portfolio if you're drowning in debt.

You can't foster a loving relationship if you haven't forgiven last month's fight.

You can't lay a foundation if there's a pile of rubble.

Surveying your land is sacred preparation. You have to clean up the overgrowth before you start to build.

Most people skip this step because it feels too painful. Taking inventory and cleaning up your life often stirs negative emotions, like shame, resentment, and regret, especially if your life feels like a mess. To truly expand your life into something abundant, you cannot skip this step.

Your Past Doesn't Define You

When you begin surveying the land of your life, you may not like what you see. It's painful to admit that you had an active role in the breakdown of your marriage, your financial mess, or your excess weight. It feels awful not having anything to show for your time on earth.

Without realizing it, we've been conditioned to believe that our actions define who we are. If you fail a test, you're a failure. If you forget an answer, you're stupid. If you get rejected from a job, you're a loser. We believe our identity is linked directly to our actions.

This is where the evil of perfectionism comes from. You begin to tell yourself that if you can just do and be perfect in all things, then you'll be good enough, which doesn't leave room for mistakes. When your actions, good or bad, define you as a person, shame shows up when you get it wrong.

Shame attacks your identity. It says your mistake defines you. Shame convinces you that the weeds and crumbling fences are evidence that you're flawed and defective, but shame is wrong.

You're not a collection of your past choices, beliefs, wounds, or reactions. You did the best you could with what you knew. You made decisions from the awareness you had, the wounds you carried, and the tools you were given. You may have been immature, afraid, or coping.

Your actions don't define you. You're formed from dust, but you're defined by the Divine within you.

On the other hand, if your identify isn't determined by your actions, when you make a mistake, you'll experience a different emotion — guilt.

Guilt addresses your behavior without identifying with it. You don't need to judge yourself harshly because your mistake doesn't change your worth. Guilt alerts you that your action was off so you can correct it, restore it, and grow from it.

Shame whispers, *You are the mistake. You are the failure. You are flawed.*

Guilt says, *You made a mistake. You can learn. You are growing.*

Shame condemns. Guilt guides. Shame keeps you stuck in

a false identity, while guilt invites you to take responsibility and move forward with integrity.

Here you are, standing on your plot of land. It's the dawn of a new day. You're not the person you were yesterday. Your eyes are opening, your awareness is expanding, and your mind is transforming.

If you need to repair what you broke, repair it. If you need to repay a debt, repay it. If you need to confess to poor behavior, confess it. But don't let a past action define you.

You're not your weeds.

You're not your rubble.

You're not your worst moment.

You are His dwelling place.

Release judgment, and be gentle with yourself, because you did the best you could with what you knew.

You know more now, so you can build differently.

Healing the Land with Compassion

This land, your inner world, has carried both your joy and your heartbreak. It's seen your highest hopes and deepest regrets, and still it holds you.

Combating shame so you can heal your land begins with compassion.

Compassion wraps your mistakes, shortcomings, and regrets in a blanket of grace. Compassion doesn't pretend everything is fine or excuse the past. It doesn't ignore natural consequences. Instead, it chooses gentleness without condemning.

Your past self did what she could to survive and make it through. She wasn't trying to ruin your future. She was doing her best. Thank her for that. Forgive her for not always getting it right.

Everything you did in your past brought you to this moment, and you were made for a time such as this.

Judgment chains you to the past. Compassion frees you to grow.

Because you choose to rise from the rubble and heal your land, today, you'll live in abundance tomorrow.

You Are on Holy Ground

I once heard someone say that when you ask God to move the mountain, he usually hands you a shovel.

The shovel is the work that is yours to do. It's God saying, *You're capable. Let's begin.*

You may be standing in front of your mountain of regret, and now you're holding a shovel. All your mistakes loom over you, taunting you from the past. It can feel like God has abandoned you as you stare at your impossible task.

But you're not working alone, for even in the work of clearing the land, you're partnering with the Divine. On the back side of the mountain, He's at work, too. For every shovel you move in Love, He's moving with a backhoe.

Before you begin, bend low and take off your shoes, for you are working on holy ground, not because the soil beneath you is sacred, but because you are.

The Divine lives in your breath, your heartbeat, and your bones. He came close, breathing Life—His Life—into you. He shared His essence with you, making you in His image, making you holy.

Every step you take consecrates the earth. This is your

burning bush, the moment when the ordinary becomes holy. You're the temple where heaven dwells. You are the holy ground.

Keep your shovel steady. Let the flame wrap around you, as you listen for the guiding voice that comes from within.

From this holy ground, prepare to build.

AFFIRMATION

"I am holy ground because the Divine is within me."

PART 4

BUILDING FROM THE INSIDE OUT

THE KINGDOM OF GOD WITHIN

13

THE KINGDOM IS WITHIN

PRAYER

"You're the light that fills my soul and the peace that anchors my heart."

The Kingdom of God

Standing on a hillside surrounded by crowds of ordinary people, Jesus said, "The kingdom of God is within you."

He didn't point to a temple, a throne in the sky, or a mountain where God dwells. He pointed to you.

We often search for God outside ourselves, whether in good deeds, relationships, church buildings, or spiritual experiences. We chase signs and proof, not realizing the very thing we seek has been quietly waiting within us all along.

The Source of your power, meaning, and purpose isn't out there in some mystical place where you must find Him. No, everything you need to build an abundant life is already within you.

This is the secret that was hidden from humanity for thousands of years, but Jesus came to reveal where we meet God face to face.

If the kingdom is within you, how do you access it? How do you live from it?

To understand the kingdom within, you must first understand the One who reigns there. The nature of the kingdom can only be known through the nature of its King.

Why Our Image of God Matters

Most of us believe in God, but how each of us interprets Him or describes Him is often very different. We assume we're all on the same page, but we actually don't all believe the same things about Him.

If I describe God as a good friend, you may imagine someone who calls often and shows up consistently, while someone else may picture a person who calls occasionally to catch up on life.

If I say God is a loving Father, you may think of warmth and constant affection, while someone else imagines a distant authority who provides but rarely comforts.

These differences matter more than we realize.

Our personal experiences shape how we define God. Because of our vast array of experiences, our definitions vary as much as our experiences. In a room of 100 people, you'll get 100 different experiences with a father. This creates inconsistent descriptions of God from one person to the next, and this breeds confusion.

I want to take a moment to establish a concise definition of God to get us on the same page, so we can speak the same language that evokes the same unified image of the Divine.

To be very clear, I don't claim to understand everything about God. How could any of us? The Infinite cannot be contained by language or doctrine.

But I do know this much: there is no fear in God. Fear is not His language, and confusion is not His way.

In clarifying the image of God, I hope to help lift the fog that surrounds Him and dissolve the fear that's followed you into your faith by awakening what your spirit already knows.

When something is true and aligned with God, you don't always need words for it. You recognize it like brushing the hem of His garment. It feels alive and known.

Trust that knowing. Lean into it.

As false images of God begin to fall away, something holy is unveiled. You'll stop striving to reach Him and begin resting in Him. Fear will loosen its grip, anxiety will quiet, and peace will awaken.

From that place, you can finally begin to build on a foundation that does not shift.

God Is Love

After stripping away every distorted image and every conflicting description of God, I set out to find the most foundational definition possible.

We don't need an interpretation or a lengthy theological essay. We don't need to define Him through a cultural or religious lens. What we need is a definition that's universal and unshakable. We need an image that every human heart can recognize.

When you peel back all the layers, one truth remains: God is Love.

You can't get more fundamental than that.

God is Love.

Sit with that for a few months and let it sink into your soul. God isn't a loving God.

No, God is Love itself.

Let's take it one step further. There's a simple principle in mathematics that says if A equals B, then B equals A.

When applied to the Divine, that means, if God is Love, then Love is God.

God and Love aren't separate. They're the same. To experience Love is to experience God. To express Love is to express God.

Using this simple definition to describe God dissipates the foggy confusion of religious jargon and ambiguous meanings around God. It gives us a clear foundation to begin building our lives on.

But like God, Love is vastly misunderstood. Love is tossed around casually to describe a fond affection for people, animals, and inanimate objects. You love your morning coffee, your neighbor's puppy, and the people dearest to you. We use the word so loosely that it's lost much of its meaning.

Now, I want to take a moment to define Love to strengthen our collective image of God.

Defining Love

Divine Love isn't butterflies or fleeting emotions. It isn't born from physical attraction or chemistry. Love isn't a human feeling at all, no, it's God Himself, the sacred current that flows through all and in all. It's the unseen thread that ties the world together. Love is the steady heartbeat of creation itself.

You can find Love's pure and unchanging character in the scripture's love chapter.

Love isn't rushed. Instead, He moves with quiet patience, allowing life to unfold in time. He doesn't push or demand, but waits, steady as the sunrise. Love is kind and gentle.

Love has no envy in Him, but celebrates others' joy as if it were His own, knowing that abundance is never diminished when shared.

Love honors others. He listens, and his voice is soft. He gives unconditionally and doesn't keep score. He forgives.

Love isn't self-seeking. He doesn't demand that we acknowledge He's first or right, because He already knows this about Himself, and our lack of understanding doesn't change that.

He can bow low, as Jesus demonstrated, and still know His worth. He's not easily angered because He sees through the eyes of compassion, understanding humanity is dust.

Love rejoices in what's true and refuses to distort or hide behind deceit. Instead, He protects what is sacred, guards what is vulnerable, and builds where others might tear down.

Love always trusts, not blindly, but faithfully. He sees the best in others and believes in redemption. He always hopes and never stops showing up.

You'll find Love in the patience of a friend, the kindness of a stranger, and the stillness within your own heart. Empires may crumble, and stars may fade, but Love remains.

Love never fails, for Love is God.

As you gain clarity on the nature of Love, you'll have your North Star to guide you. Love reveals who God is, and when you understand His character, you understand how to walk in alignment with Him.

For example, if you find yourself rushed and desperate for something to happen, pause and reflect. Those feelings signal that you've stepped out of alignment with Love, because Love is patient. The moment you choose to quiet your mind, release control, and trust the unfolding, you return to the divine flow. In that stillness, you move back into harmony with God's will, where everything unfolds in its perfect time.

Now that we have a clear, simple definition of God, we can understand the kingdom of God and how to access it.

Building from the Inside Out

You can't access the kingdom of Love through your circumstances. The kingdom of Love is within you, and the doorway to access it is your mind.

There is no other way.

You're not just flesh and bone reacting to the world around you. You're a thinking substance. You have an inner chamber animated by your spirit that only you have access to, and it's from this chamber that you produce thoughts, and from your thoughts flow your words, actions, and ultimately your life.

Your mind is a sacred temple, a holy cathedral, and it's in this secret place that you and God meet. Your vision is born there. Your imagination is housed there. Your faith lives there. Love resides there.

To build from God's kingdom means your Source of truth lives within your mind, not in the outside world. Your inner world determines how you interpret and respond to everything around you.

Most people live the opposite way. They live from the outside in, allowing the outer world to dictate their inner world.

If the bank account is low, they believe they're broke.

If the marriage is struggling, they believe they're unloved.

If life feels unstable, they believe God has abandoned them.

Their five senses are their master. What they see, hear, and feel determines what they believe. Their mood rises and falls with headlines. Their worth shifts with opinions. Their peace depends on outcomes.

When your senses are your Source of truth, your life is built on sand. Every storm shakes you. Every setback threatens you. Every delay feels like a punishment.

But Jesus told us the wise builder builds on the rock. The rock isn't your circumstances, it's the kingdom of Love within.

To live from the inside out means your identity, security, and peace are rooted in Love before the evidence supports it. It means you choose to live according to a higher truth over the report of your senses. You live by faith.

This is the upside-down kingdom.

To human logic, it looks foolish. It doesn't make sense to speak peace in the middle of chaos, and you sound crazy declaring health when you have a fever and a cough.

Living from the inside out is the hardest work you'll ever do, because it requires faith. You must deny what your eyes see, what your ears hear, and what your hands touch, and instead trust a higher Truth.

It doesn't mean you live in denial. It means that you recognize the Divine within is the cause, and your outer world is the effect.

Building your life from Love doesn't mean everything will be perfect. It means when storms come, you remain grounded, because Love is the rock you build on.

You build this inner kingdom through quiet, consistent choices that flow from thoughts rooted in Love rather than fear. Each time you forgive, speak truth, create beauty, or show kindness, that's Love expanding through you. That's another stone in your cathedral.

And over time, your outer life begins to mirror your inner one. What you build internally in Love will begin to manifest outwardly in relationships, work, and life.

Starting today, seek this kingdom first, turning inward to the holy cathedral within. There, in stillness, you'll find the King, Love Himself, waiting to reign.

AFFIRMATION

"The kingdom of God is within me. Love lives in me and breathes through me."

14

YOUR THOUGHTS CREATE YOUR REALITY

PRAYER

"Help me to become a faithful gatekeeper of my mind."

The Power of Your Thoughts

Everything in your physical world began as a thought.

Take a moment and look around the room you're in right now. Everything your eyes land on, the chair you're sitting in, the phone in your hand, the lamp in the corner, even this very book, first existed as an idea in someone's mind.

Before the first cathedral stone is laid, it stands complete in the architect's mind. Before the first business opens its doors, it lives in the imagination of its founder. Before a marriage is healed, restoration must first be an inner vision.

Everything starts in the mind.

Even humanity itself began this way.

Before your first breath, He saw your unformed body. You began as a divine thought before you became human flesh.

This isn't poetic language. It's a pattern. Everything created follows in the same order, and this law governs your life, as well.

It's through your thoughts that you create your reality. Your mind has a creative power that no other living creature has. You have the capacity to form an image that does not exist in the outer world.

We call this power imagination. It's from your imagination that you mold your life.

This is the natural law of creation. The natural progression goes like this. First, there's a thought. Then, belief. Then, action. It's your action that produces the physical form.

Earl Nightingale famously said, "You become what you think about."

The thoughts you continually dwell on shape your beliefs. What shapes your beliefs begins to influence your decisions. Your decisions shape your habits, and your habits build your life.

Your life today is the physical reflection of the thoughts you consistently entertained in your past.

That's how creation works, and that's how your life is built.

Your Mind Is Your Greatest Treasure

Your mind is the temple where the Divine meets your humanity. It's your inner cathedral where God dwells, and no one else has access to it but you. No one can think your thoughts or know your mind. Its capacity for growth and expansion is staggering and still being studied. It's capable of so much more than we know.

Yet, most people treat their minds carelessly. They leave it unguarded, unattended, and uncultivated.

They allow headlines, social media, fear, comparison, resentment, and old wounds to plant seeds freely. They rehearse past failures. They imagine worst-case scenarios. They replay insults and feed their anxieties, then wonder why their lives feel overwhelming and chaotic.

Your mind is like a garden, and your thoughts are its seeds. Whatever you plant will grow.

Philosophers, scholars, and teachers throughout history have repeated this truth in different forms. The Roman emperor Marcus Aurelius wrote that our thoughts shape our lives. Emerson observed that a person becomes what he thinks about all day. The language varies, but the message remains the same: what you think, you become.

Scripture echoes it just as clearly. "As a man thinks in his heart, so is he." We're told to set our minds on things above and to think on whatever is true, noble, and right.

Yet, so many people don't understand this important truth. Earl Nightingale called it "the strangest secret" because even though it's not a secret, very few people actually know what to do with their pearl of great price.

Abundance isn't found in money, paychecks, or a 401 (k). It's not the home you live in, the car you drive, or the brands you wear. These are the things that most people put high value on, but they're replaceable. They could all burn up today and easily be replaced tomorrow.

Your mind, on the other hand, was given for free at birth, and we rarely put high value on free gifts, but it's within this gift that lies the source of true abundance. It's in your ability to think and imagine. Abundance is the endless creative flow of ideas, intelligence, and wisdom that flows from Love. All the money in the world cannot replace a mind once it's gone.

You must seek first the kingdom of Love. Obsessively, compulsively seek the inner kingdom first, and all these things — money, possessions, and provisions — will be added unto you. They're added as you exchange your creative thoughts and intelligence for material income.

If you don't awaken to the power of your mind and take control of it, your unattended mind will take control and enslave you to emotional and spiritual turmoil.

Awaken to the treasure you carry. Guard it, cultivate it, and revere it, because from this place, your entire life is built.

You're the Gatekeeper

If your mind is a garden, then you're its gatekeeper.

You, the thinking substance, are the one who controls the health and well-being of your garden. No one can access your mind, so it's not up to anyone else to take care of it. Even though God has access, he isn't one to manipulate and control. He quietly waits in the cool of the day, ready to walk alongside you, whenever you're ready.

Most of us were never taught how to gatekeep our minds. No one explained how to control your thoughts, so your thoughts control you instead. Any and all thoughts run through your mind like wild boars, ripping and rooting out your garden. Vines of fear, anxiety, and depression weave through your mind, wrapping themselves around your heart, squeezing out happiness and joy.

You feel like you're going crazy as panic and stress beat up your body, leaving you in a sweaty, tearful heap on the floor. Every waking minute, your past torments you, and future worst-case scenarios haunt your dreams. Worry grows freely, choking out peace.

You pray to God to take control, to free you from your pain, but it feels like your prayers fall on deaf ears. Just know He has heard you. He's just patiently waiting with your shovel.

You control your thoughts. Your thoughts don't control you. But if you've spent your entire life allowing your thoughts to run unchecked, it's going to feel absolutely impossible to take control.

You can't control what thoughts pop into your head, but you control how long they live there. You decide which thoughts you allow to take root and which you'll pull out and toss. Good or bad, Love or fear, flowers or weeds, what you allow to stay in your mind will grow a bountiful harvest. What you sow, you will reap.

Pull the Weeds and Kick out the Boars

Pulling the weeds and kicking out the negative wild boars is going to be the hardest work you'll ever do. I know I keep saying this, but I want to make sure you release the false idea that establishing the kingdom of Love within you is easy work. It's not. It's work that requires daily dying to your old self, and some days it's going to feel like one step forward, 10 steps back.

Getting control of your thoughts is like clearing gnomes from a garden in *Harry Potter*. You pull them out and toss them over the wall, only to watch them crawl right back in. So you pull them out again. And again. And again.

That's what it feels like to uproot fear. You'll throw it out in the morning and find it burrowing back in by afternoon. It's exhausting.

But if you don't do this mental work, fear stays and burrows deep, poisoning the soil.

It won't always be this difficult. Fearful thoughts weaken each time you toss them out. Each time you refuse to let them in, they lose power. Eventually, they won't have the strength to climb the wall. You'll see them knocking at the gate, begging you to let them in, but by then, it will be easy to say no.

Your reality is the product of the thoughts that live in your mind. To change your life, you must change your thoughts.

Your life isn't random. It's being built, thought by thought. You're not powerless or a victim of your mind.

You're its gatekeeper, and from this day forward, cultivate it with intention.

AFFIRMATION

"My thoughts become my reality. I am the gatekeeper of my mind."

15

TAP INTO THE MIND OF LOVE

PRAYER

"Give me the strength to rewrite the false stories I've believed for too long."

***

Your Two Minds

As you become the gatekeeper of your mind, your goal is to root your thoughts in Love. God's will is expanding in Love and that starts in your mind. Understanding how your mind operates will help in transforming your thoughts.

Science tells us we operate with two levels of mind: the conscious and the subconscious.

Your conscious mind is the thinking mind. It's the part of you that reasons, analyzes, plans, and makes deliberate choices. It's what you're using right now as you read these words. But it's limited. It can focus on only a small amount of information at a time.

Beneath it lies your far more powerful subconscious mind. If the conscious mind is the screen, the subconscious is the operating system running behind it.

Your subconscious stores every memory, belief, and emotional pattern you've ever experienced. It operates the functions of your body, so you don't have to think about breathing, blinking, or swallowing. It shapes your habits, guides your reactions, and influences your behavior without asking for permission.

Most of your daily life isn't directed by conscious thought. It flows from what has already been programmed into your subconscious.

This matters because your subconscious doesn't filter for truth. It doesn't argue, analyze, or question what you give it. It simply accepts repetition as instruction.

If you continually repeat fear, it builds patterns around fear.

If you meditate on Love, it operates from Love.

Your subconscious is like the most obedient assistant you've ever had. What you repeatedly tell it, it will faithfully file away in your subconscious mind. Whether your thoughts are rooted in fear or Love, it doesn't care. It'll program them into your belief system as truth. It simply follows your lead.

Which means the life you're building is being shaped by your deep subconscious beliefs, not what you consciously know.

It's Not What You Know, It's What You Believe

What makes understanding your subconscious beliefs difficult is that they're buried deep in the recesses of your mind, making it hard for your conscious, thinking mind to access them. Your conscious mind pulls up concrete knowledge you know is true, but that knowledge isn't actually your deep-seated belief.

For example, you may consciously know that eating too many sweets isn't healthy. You can explain how sugar affects your body. You've read the articles. You understand the long-term consequences. If someone asked you, "Is this good for you?" you would confidently say no.

That's conscious knowledge.

But imagine you've had a stressful day. You feel overwhelmed, unseen, and exhausted. Without thinking much about it, you reach for cookies or ice cream.

At that moment, your behavior isn't being driven by your conscious knowledge about nutrition. It's driven by a subconscious belief.

Maybe somewhere deep inside you believe, *sugar comforts me.* Or, *I deserve this.* Or, *this is the only thing that makes me feel better.*

Your conscious mind knows one thing, but your subconscious mind believes another, and belief will always overpower knowledge.

The same thing happens in relationships. You may consciously know that you're worthy of love. You can say the words out loud. You can quote Scripture about your identity in Christ. But if your subconscious belief is, "I'm not enough," you'll interpret a person's frustration as rejection. You'll overanalyze their tone, body language, and intentions. You'll constantly brace for abandonment.

Your life follows what you believe, not what you know.

If truth hasn't moved from conscious knowledge into

subconscious belief, your old programming will continue to run the show. This is why you sometimes act against your own better judgment. It's what Paul meant when he said, "For what I want to do I do not do, but what I hate I do."

Your conflicting behavior doesn't mean you're weak. It's just that your subconscious beliefs, formed in childhood, shaped by trauma, or written by culture, are running the show.

The way you rewrite your programming is by becoming deeply aware of what's happening in your inner world. It begins with paying close attention to your thoughts, words, and actions in every situation. They reveal your beliefs.

This kind of awareness is how you stop letting the old programming dictate the shape of your life and start intentionally designing the structure you want to build.

Think About What You Think About

Most people never stop to examine their thoughts.

They wake up and immediately react. They react to the news, to their spouse, to the traffic. They're constantly reacting to stress and disappointments. Their day is a string of automatic reactions, driven by old programming they've never questioned.

They live on autopilot. Life happens, and they react.

To truly live tapped into the mind of Love, you must stop reacting to life and instead begin creating, responding intentionally, and building with purpose.

The first step to gaining control of your mind is to think about what you think about. This will bring awareness to whether your beliefs are rooted in fear or Love.

Slow down and observe your inner dialogue.

What runs through your mind when something goes wrong?

How do you speak to yourself when you make a mistake?

What assumptions do you instantly make about others?

What story are you telling yourself about life?

You can also listen to your spoken words. Your speech reveals your beliefs, because out of the abundance of the heart the mouth speaks.

If you constantly say, "Nothing ever works out for me," your words reveal that you believe God is working against you. If you speak down about yourself, it shows you don't believe you deserve kindness and respect.

Your outward expressions expose your inner beliefs.

Awareness is the doorway to change. You cannot uproot a weed you don't know is there. This is part of your preparation to build. The moment you begin paying attention, you shift out of autopilot and into empowerment.

When you start noticing your thoughts instead of being ruled by them, you've taken the first step in taking your garden back.

Choose Love

You were given the knowledge of good and evil. Through your imagination, you have the power to create thoughts that are either rooted in Love or fear. You always have the choice of what you'll create.

There's no neutral ground. It's always either Love or fear, light or darkness.

Fear is the master of the material world. It believes truth is what you see, touch, and feel. It spends its time reacting to life's circumstances, living as a ship tossed around by every storm. It rules with anxiety, worry, and stress.

Love is the master of the spiritual world. It defines reality by what is known within. It's not ruled by appearances but anchored in unseen laws. Love doesn't deny the storms; it sleeps in the belly of the ship. It rules with peace, kindness, and joy.

Fear contracts. Love expands.

Fear is darkness. Love is light.

Fear is chaos. Love is order.

Fear builds on sand. Love builds on the rock.

You cannot build with both present in your mind. You're either building with fear, or you're building with Love. You can't serve two masters. You must either cling to one and reject the other. You can only choose one.

You can't say you're living in light while you continually plant darkness.

Creation is orderly. The harvest always matches the seed planted.

Choose thoughts rooted in Love, in every moment and in every situation, because Love is the source from which all good things flow. The more you think from Love, the more your life will reflect it.

Guard your mind with reverence.

When a thought enters, ask yourself: Is this rooted in Love or in fear?

If you hear or see something in culture, media, or even a pulpit that stirs fear, immediately reject it from your mind, walk away, and slam the gate closed, because fear is not of God.

Choose Love.

Again and again, choose Love.

Thought Stopping

Once you learn to recognize a thought rooted in fear, the next step is learning how to stop it.

One practice is called thought stopping.

When you notice a fear-based thought pattern, you interrupt it. You stop it in its tracks.

Some people imagine a large red stop sign. I picture pulling the emergency brake on a runaway train. However you visualize it, the goal is to break the momentum before it takes control.

Then, you replace the thought with one rooted in Love and truth.

Simple in theory. Extremely difficult in practice, because most people don't realize that we get a strange sense of fulfillment from fearful thinking.

Fear is high-energy. Stress feels urgent. Worry feels responsible. When you're replaying worst-case scenarios, it can feel like you're caring. When you're obsessing over finances, anxious conversations can feel productive. When you're scanning for danger, it can feel like protection.

But fear rarely moves you into creative, productive action. It drains you and keeps you disconnected from God, because light and darkness can't co-exist.

Thought stopping feels unnatural at first because your nervous system has grown accustomed to the rush.

I learned this one night when I woke from a nightmare that our house was on fire, and I couldn't reach my children.

My body was shaking, and my heart was pounding. It felt so real that I began to cry.

Even after I was fully awake, my mind kept replaying the scene, making it worse each time. I imagined screaming as the fire consumed my house with my children in it.

I've practiced thought stopping for years, but in that moment, I didn't want to stop. It felt like love. It felt like a mother protecting her children.

But the truth was that there was no fire. My children were safe. The danger existed only in an imaginary story my mind had created. It wasn't real. My panic was wreaking havoc by catapulting me out of Love and into the dark abyss of fear.

Several minutes passed before I finally pulled the brake and stopped the spiral. It took great effort to get control, slow my breathing, and ground my thoughts in Love. *My children are safe. There isn't a fire. This is an imaginary story rooted in fear.*

It's taking control and choosing Love over fear. It's believing truth over imagined stories. This is the only way you can overcome.

You won't get it right every time. Some nights, fear will win. Some days, it will take several attempts, but every time you stop a fear-based thought and replace it with Love, you weaken fear's authority.

You reclaim your mind and lay another stone in a cathedral built on the rock.

Daily Renew Your Mind

Reprogramming your mind isn't a one-time event. Instead, it's a daily practice, a continual renewing of your mind. It's what Paul meant when he said to inwardly renew day by day. Each day, you must die to the beliefs of fear, shame, and limitation, and replace them with divine truth. You repeat the new script until it becomes second nature. You teach your subconscious a new system.

The true and lasting transformation begins when you learn to tap into the higher consciousness of the mind of Love. It's here that the false stories lose their power. It's here that you align your thoughts with truth and build a life that reflects who you truly are.

Close your eyes for a moment and imagine what might unfold if you truly believed Love was building with you. What if you believed that God desires to manifest Himself through you? Imagine the weight that would fall from your shoulders if you stopped trying to earn your worth and allowed Love to flow from the inside out. Oh, that you would see that this is the Father's greatest pleasure!

This is the invitation to become not just a builder, but a co-creator with Love. To tear down the crumbling walls of fear and shame, and lay a new foundation on truth. To stop living as a prisoner to unconscious patterns and instead choose, with every thought, to live free in Love.

The cathedral you're meant to build already exists in the mind of Love. Your work is to align your mind with His so you can bring His will into the visible world around you.

AFFIRMATION

"I choose to root my thoughts in Love."

16

YOU'RE SO EMOTIONAL

PRAYER

"Help me listen to my emotions with curiosity instead of fear."

Emotional Crisis

"I'm sorry, I don't know what's wrong with me. I can't stop crying. I never cry like this."

I waited quietly as my client, on the other side of our video call, wiped her cheeks, trying to hold back the emotional dam that was breaking.

As a marriage coach, I've watched both men and women battle shame and fear around their natural emotional response to their suffering. I'm full of compassion because I remember my own fear and shame.

Today, millions of people are struggling with their emotional health. In 2020, the CDC reported that approximately 42 million adult Americans are taking medication for depression, anxiety, or other mental health conditions each year. And the numbers continue to increase.

These statistics reveal just how much people are hurting, but deeper still, the statistics reveal that we don't understand our emotions or what to do with the pain we carry inside.

Negative emotions are the hardest for us to deal with. When someone cries too much, when sadness lingers too long, or when anger explodes too aggressively, we panic, especially when there isn't a visible crisis to justify it.

We're told you're not supposed to feel this way.

So you spring into action, trying to get over it. Dry your tears, think happy thoughts, and plaster on a smile. Stuff, ignore, and pretend. You attempt to stay afloat, trying to control the raging waves inside of you. Eventually, exhaustion sets in, and you panic as the darkness pulls you under.

We're living in an emotional crisis.

But the crisis exists because we're fighting the wrong battle. We're trying to control the wrong thing.

Your emotions aren't the enemy.

In fact, they're one of the most important gifts you've ever given.

Emotions are a Gift

There's nothing wrong or bad about your emotions. They're a very natural and vital part of the human experience.

They're the alert system to your inner being.

Think about the role your nervous system plays in your body. If you accidentally touch a hot stove, pain shoots through your hand and into your brain. That pain isn't your enemy. It's a signal telling you something is wrong. Without it, you wouldn't recognize that your body was in danger.

Emotions work the same way in your inner world.

They signal when something within you needs attention. They tell you when what you're experiencing feels safe, joyful, threatening, painful, or out of alignment.

Sadness signals loss or disappointment.

Fear warns you that you may be unsafe.

Happiness alerts you that you're aligned and well.

Instead of labeling emotions as good or bad, begin to see them simply as positive and negative. Neither is bad nor wrong to experience. We need them all to live abundantly. They're all good and natural.

Emotions aren't your enemy that you need to suppress or control. They're signals to help you understand what's going on inside of you.

Why We're Afraid of Our Emotions

You learned about emotions by watching the people around you, and what most of us witnessed was emotional chaos.

Maybe you grew up around explosive emotions. You saw aggressive anger with screaming, breaking objects, and slamming doors. Emotions were an unpredictable roller coaster of extreme highs and lows. You learned they were violent and frightening, weapons that hurt people.

Or maybe you grew up around the opposite — suppressed emotions. You saw anger in harsh words through gritted teeth, in silent treatment, and in withdrawn affection. Emotions simmered quietly for days. You learned they were dangerous and unsafe, and needed to be locked away.

Over time, you begin to associate emotions with aggression, loss of control, or punishment.

What you were actually witnessing were wounded emotions, not healthy ones.

Healthy emotions move through us, teaching us what needs to change, heal, or adjust. Unhealthy emotions stay trapped, spiraling unproductively.

When you learn to trust and process emotions, they begin to feel like a safe, supportive friend.

Your Thoughts Control Your Emotions

Emotions feel powerful, but they're not in charge of your inner world.

Your thoughts are.

What you think decides what you feel. Your emotions are the natural response to whatever you're thinking about. You think a thought, and your emotional alert system fires off a response.

This happens with every thought you have throughout the day. Most thoughts pass through your mind quietly and carry little meaning, so your emotional response stays neutral. But when a thought carries deeper meaning, like judgment, fear, disappointment, loss, or excitement, your emotional system responds with equal intensity. The stronger the thought, the stronger the feeling that follows.

This is why our emotions are unfairly blamed for our internal chaos. We're constantly trying to control how we're feeling when all it's doing is responding to what you're thinking about.

Our emotions are like the little sister being quietly teased by her older brother. For a long time, she tries to ignore it. She tolerates the poking and the comments. But eventually she reaches her limit and lashes out.

Suddenly, the parents rush in and scold her for the outburst, because they never noticed what the brother had been saying all along.

This is how most people treat their emotions.

We rush in to punish the emotional reaction without ever examining the thoughts that provoked it. Your thoughts constantly whisper messages in your mind, and if they repeat themselves enough, your emotions will respond.

Habitual thoughts create habitual emotions. Over time, repeated thoughts can turn temporary emotions into long-term emotional states. Continual thoughts rooted in fear create chronic anxiety and depression. Thoughts rooted in resentment produce ongoing bitterness. Thoughts rooted in gratitude and Love cultivate lasting peace and joy.

Your emotional state is constantly being shaped by the thoughts running through your mind.

It may appear that outside circumstances or others cause you to feel a certain way, but it's the thought you have about the person or the circumstance that causes your emotional response. It's still your thought that made you feel that way, not the outside experience.

Your thought, then emotional response, happens almost instantly, so you don't even realize it's happening. Your senses take in the world around you, and your mind immediately begins interpreting what it means. In the brief moment between the event and the emotion, your mind forms a judgment, expectation, or interpretation about what just happened. It's your interpretation that produces the emotion.

No one can make you feel a certain way.

This is why two people can experience the same situation and experience two different emotions. It's because they had different thoughts about it.

If you don't like what you are feeling, pause and ask yourself an honest question: *What thoughts am I thinking?*

Emotions Need to be Processed, Not Controlled

Emotions are a temporary energy that, just like blood, needs to flow. Blocked emotions are dangerous.

When emotions are allowed to move through you, they eventually pass, but when they're blocked, they don't disappear. They remain trapped inside the body and mind, leaking out in other ways like irritability, exhaustion, anxiety, insomnia, or even physical illness. Research continues to show strong links between emotional suppression and problems like chronic stress, immune system dysfunction, and anxiety disorders.

Your emotions need to be processed, not controlled.

Neuroscientist Dr. Jill Bolte Taylor says that when an emotional reaction is triggered, the physical response lasts about ninety seconds. That's it. It takes less than two minutes for your body to process anger, frustration, and excitement when you let them flow.

She also explains that any emotion that continues is usually sustained by our thoughts about what happened.

In other words, emotions are designed to pass through

you quickly when you allow them to flow. The problem is that most of us were never taught how to let them pass. Instead, we either fight our emotions or try to shut them down completely. We tighten up, distract ourselves, or pretend we're fine, and the emotional energy stays trapped inside.

Learning how to process emotions is a skill. Like any skill, it can be practiced and strengthened.

Here's a simple way to begin.

How to Process Negative Emotions

If you've spent years blocking, suppressing, and exploding your uncomfortable emotions, it's time to begin allowing yourself to feel them fully and process them properly.

It's important to know that you can't block one emotion without blocking them all. When you shut down anger, sadness, or frustration, you also dull your capacity for joy, peace, and happiness, because the same emotional system that allows you to feel sadness also allows you to feel joy.

1. Accept Your Emotions

Your emotions aren't wrong. They're signals informing you that something inside you needs attention. You're not supposed to force yourself to feel a certain way all the time. Give all your emotions permission to show up as they come.

Release the habit of feeling guilty for what you feel.

"I'm allowed to feel this way."

2. Name the Emotion

Pause and name the emotion. Naming it helps your brain gain clarity on the inner chaos you may be experiencing.

"I'm feeling __________ (angry, hurt, anxious, nervous), and that's ok."

3. Express Emotions Safely

Emotions are energy moving through the body. They need a safe outlet.

People are often terrified to open the door to their emotions because it feels as if the flood will never stop. The grief will be endless. The anger will consume them. The sadness will pull them under. But your emotions aren't an ocean you'll drown in. They're a puddle. When you dare to step in and sit with them, you discover they move through you and pass. The feeling rises, swells for a moment, and then begins to fade. You won't drown in your emotions. All they're asking is that you stop avoiding long enough to sit in the puddle and listen to what they have to tell you.

You can express it by crying, screaming into a pillow, or journaling. Take a walk. Sit quietly and breathe. Let the feeling rise and pass.

When expressing intense emotions, like anger, here are three non-negotiables:

1. Do not harm yourself.
2. Do not harm others.
3. Do not destroy property.

If you're processing deeper emotions caused by trauma, abuse, or death, they will last longer and surface with greater intensity. You don't have to live with that emotional door wide open. Open it for as long as you can, then close it for a while to let yourself recover. Just don't be afraid to open the door, because each time you do, the intensity will lessen.

4. Identify the Thought That Triggered the Emotion

Ask yourself what belief or interpretation triggered the feeling.

What thought was I just thinking that created this feeling?

What thoughts did I think after the experience that made me feel this way?

Is this thought actually true, or is it a story my mind is creating?

Is it rooted in Love or fear?

5. Resolve It

Once you express the emotion and identify the thoughts behind it, don't leave the situation hanging. Emotional health requires resolution.

Sometimes resolution involves action with others, and sometimes it involves changing your thinking.

How can I reframe my thoughts to align with truth and Love?

Do I need to heal the situation with someone?

6. Release It

Once you feel, process, and resolve your emotion, it's time to let it go.

One of the most self-destructive habits is allowing past experiences to play on repeat in your mind. Become the gate-keeper and take control of your thoughts. Don't allow yourself to continue to replay it, and don't carry it into the next moment.

"I release this moment, and I commit to not revisiting it."

Feel it. Learn from it. Release it.

Your emotions have been sending you important messages your entire life. Don't punish them. Listen to them. They're such an important gift to help you learn more about the kingdom within.

You're an incredible human who's been given such a sacred task of building an emotionally grounded cathedral in Love.

Keep going, you're doing good work.

AFFIRMATION

"I honor my emotions. They're my teacher."

PART 5

THERE'S MORE THAN ENOUGH TO BUILD

ABUNDANCE MINDSET

17

ABUNDANCE ABOUNDS

PRAYER

"Open my eyes to Your abundance all around me. Teach me to align myself with it."

Our Abundant Universe

You live in an abundant universe.

Everywhere you look, life overflows. Forests teem with trees, each with countless branches covered in leaves. Rivers flow without end, and stars are too many to count. Even beneath your feet, billions of tiny organisms grow. The pattern of creation is constant expansion.

Think of an apple seed. From one small seed grows a tree that produces hundreds of apples. Each apple holds more seeds — the potential for more trees. Within a single seed lives the possibility of an entire orchard.

Abundance is built into creation itself. Nature expands because it was designed to do so.

From the beginning, the command was given to be fruitful and multiply. The natural world doesn't argue with that command. It doesn't hesitate or overthink it. Trees don't doubt whether they should bear fruit. Seeds don't question whether they should sprout.

Nature fulfills the Creator's design without will or resistance. It simply follows the pattern woven into it, and faithfully declares the abundant nature of Love.

God isn't scarce or limited. He's infinite, creative, and ever-expanding.

We get a glimpse of Him when we stare into the endless night sky. You feel so insignificant when you try to comprehend how far our universe extends. If you've ever stared into the dark waters of the ocean, you've felt the uneasiness of not being able to grasp its depth.

As a child, I remember asking my mom where God came from. *Surely, He had to come from somewhere.*

She teased, "Don't think about it too hard or your brain will explode."

Our finite mind struggles to wrap itself around the Infinite.

You may never comprehend the endless, expansive nature of Love, but He shows Himself to you in your every inhale, every heartbeat, and every ray of sunshine on your skin.

Like the blossoms and the butterflies, Love seeks to express His abundant nature through you. But unlike nature, you have a choice. You can deny your design and close yourself off or open up to it.

You can choose to think in terms of abundance rather than lack.

You can choose to live from the steady overflow of Love rather than the trickle of scarcity.

You can choose to trust that the same creative force woven into the caterpillar has been placed within you.

You don't need to ask, plead, or beg God for abundance. You need to step into it.

When you align your thoughts, your beliefs, and your actions with the ever-expanding nature of Love, that's when life begins to multiply.

Scarcity Mindset vs. Abundant Mindset

When it comes to abundance, there are two fundamentally different ways of seeing the world. It's from one of these belief systems that you think, decide, give, and build. Your mindset about what is available to you will determine whether you expand in Love or shrink in fear.

One belief system is called a Scarcity Mindset, and the other is an Abundant Mindset.

A Scarcity Mindset is rooted in the material world. Seeing the world as finite, it believes there isn't enough money, love, opportunity, or time available in our universe. Because resources are limited, you must compete with others to obtain them, and once you possess them, you must cling tightly to them, lest someone steal them from you.

An Abundant Mindset, on the other hand, is rooted in the spiritual world. It sees resources as unlimited, flowing from an unseen, infinite Source. You don't need to compete for limited resources. You create from an infinite supply. You don't need to cling tightly to them, because there's always more available.

Scarcity says, "I can't afford that," while abundance says, "There's more where that came from."

Scarcity says, "There's no room for me," while abundance says, "The table keeps expanding."

Scarcity says, "There's never enough," while abundance declares, "I'm connected to an infinite supply."

You cannot build a life of expansion while thinking of limitation.

Shift into an Abundance Mindset

There's nothing holy about living in lack. You must reject the idea that it's righteous to live poor. You cannot feed the poor if you're poor. You can't give to those in need if you're in need. It's time to let go of the religious idea that insufficiency is of God. Instead, follow the lead of nature and allow Love to give to you, pressed-down, shaken together, and running over.

Position yourself in your purpose and God's will: to expand in Love. This is the what and why you're here. Then, release the how and when to the higher mind of Love.

Sit quietly until you can feel the abundant living waters rise within you. Each day, meditate on his abundance until you can feel it expand in you. Consciously commit that feeling to your subconscious mind.

You're not being greedy or selfish as you align yourself with the abundant provision, for it is the Father's great pleasure to give you his kingdom.

It's important to remember abundance isn't a collection of possessions, but a flow through you. Like water or blood, it must flow. As you freely receive, freely give. The apple tree graciously gives her fruit and shade after receiving nutrients from the soil and rays from the sun. Be careful not to adopt fear's hoarding mindset. Instead, maintain Love's flow mindset.

There's no shortage of Love. No ceiling on resources. No limit to creativity, ideas, or opportunities. The universe is abundant, and so are you. You weren't created to scrape by, but to overflow.

Open your hands and your heart and begin to build from your infinite supply until it spills over into every corner of your world.

For Love is abundance without end.

AFFIRMATION

"I live in an abundant universe. There's more than enough money, opportunities, and provision for me and everyone I love."

18

HEAL YOUR RELATIONSHIP WITH MONEY

PRAYER

"Teach me to trust in Your endless provision. Heal my false stories about money.'

Money is a Tool You Need

Money is one of the most emotionally charged topics in life, not because of what it is, but because of what we believe about it.

I think people of faith struggle the most because they're constantly trying to live in the tension between the spiritual and material worlds. Religious leaders oftentimes bring more confusion than clarity with their mixed messages. Some promote prosperity, while others teach poverty.

We hear that money is the root of all evil, that rich people are greedy, or that wanting wealth is selfish.

Many were raised in scarcity, constantly hearing phrases like, 'We can't afford that.' Or 'money doesn't grow on trees.'

Over time, those messages sink deep into your subconscious, creating resistance to receiving money. We may desire financial freedom, but on a deeper level, believe wealth is corrupt, unspiritual, or out of reach, so we push it away before it ever has a chance to come near.

The truth is that you need money to function in the world we live in. There's no way around it. It's how our society structured commerce. You can't survive without enough money to cover necessities such as housing, food, education, and healthcare.

Money isn't good or bad, holy or evil. It's a neutral tool. A hammer can build a house or destroy one, but the hammer itself isn't to blame. In the same way, money just amplifies what's already within you. If your heart is generous, wealth magnifies your ability to give. If your heart is selfish, money will magnify your greed.

To expand and grow in your life, you must heal your relationship with money. Healing begins with shifting from scarcity to abundance and from shame to stewardship.

When Money Becomes Your Source

When you live from the outside in, the material world becomes your highest truth. What you can see and measure feels most real. And in that world, money appears to be the source of everything.

Money buys the house.

Money buys the food.

Money pays the bills.

Money opens opportunities.

So it feels logical to conclude that money is the source.

From that belief, it becomes natural to chase it. To strive for it. To measure your life by it. You work for it. You worry about it. You plan around it. You stress over it. You think, *if I just had more, I'd finally feel secure.*

Money slowly becomes more than currency. It becomes your identity, safety, and worth.

In the next chapter, I'm going to talk about the parable of the rich fool, but don't be fooled. You don't need to be rich to make money your source.

Some of the most anxious, money-obsessed people aren't rich at all. They wake up every day thinking about the paycheck. They measure their value by their income. They carry constant stress about not having enough. Their thoughts revolve around lack, fear, and survival.

Just because someone doesn't have much money doesn't mean they don't serve it.

When money becomes your source, your emotional state rises and falls with your bank account. Peace is based on your deposits, and anxiety follows withdrawals. You feel abundant when numbers increase and poor when they decrease.

If your mind is constantly thinking, *what if I don't have enough?*

If your security depends on a paycheck.

If your joy depends on what you can afford.

These are signs that money has quietly taken the throne, and anything you place on the throne of your life will begin to rule you.

Ways to Heal Your Relationship with Money

Healing your relationship with money means transferring your source of abundance from material to spiritual. It's taking the power away from money and giving it to Spirit. It's putting your trust in your creative imagination, not a paycheck.

It's the daily practice of shifting your attention from the outside to the inside. It's focusing on the kingdom of Love, not the kingdom of matter.

Here are some ways you can begin healing your relationship with money.

1. Live by Faith, Not by Sight

Your current financial situation is not a reflection of your worth or your potential. It's simply a result of past thoughts, beliefs, and decisions around money. If you want your financial future to look different, you must change the way you think and speak about money today.

Begin to see with your inner eyes and hear with your inner ears. Instead of obsessing over what's in your bank account or the debts you carry, focus on aligning your mind with divine abundance. Speak words that affirm wealth, provision, and flow.

Practice replacing limiting beliefs with empowering truths:

"God is abundant, and God is my source."
"I'm grateful for the money that is flowing to me right now."

"Money flows to me and through me easily and
abundantly."
"It is the Father's good pleasure to provide for me."

2. Bless the Flow

Money is meant to circulate. Like blood in the body, air in
the lungs, or water in a river, money needs to flow to be life-
giving. If you grumble and complain about the money that
flows out of your account, you're blocking its flow back to
you. The law of abundance says that what you bless
multiplies.

Before paying a bill, pause and give thanks. Before buying
groceries or gas, offer a prayer of gratitude for the exchange
that allows your life to run smoothly. Bless the money leaving
you just as much as the money entering your hands.

Example blessings:

"I'm grateful I can exchange my time and talent for
this income."
"I bless this payment for electricity, which keeps my
home warm and bright."
"I thank God I can purchase this food that nourishes
my family."

Even when you find a coin on the ground, make it a
reminder, not of luck, but of divine provision.

As you pick it up, bless it by reading the words inscribed
on it, "In God I trust to supply my needs. Thank You for the
abundance flowing into my life."

Each small act of gratitude keeps the current of prosperity alive within you.

3. Freely Give

One of the quickest ways to heal your relationship with money is to align it with the divine law of giving and receiving. True giving isn't about putting more money in a church offering or handing out dollars in hopes that they'll come back multiplied. That's not how spiritual law works. That's how gambling works. The only place you put in a dollar expecting to get two back is at a casino.

Money is only one expression of abundance. It's not the source of it. You don't give to get. You give to expand. Giving is how you participate in the flow of creation itself.

You give more in value than you expect to receive in return. You give more than your boss asks. You give more care than is required. You give because you recognize you're not the source, but the conduit through which abundance flows.

Jesus told us when someone asks you to go one mile, go with him two. He was teaching how the law of giving and receiving works. In the measure you give, it will be given back to you. As God freely gives to you, you freely give to others.

When you give your time, energy, creativity, or resources from a full and grateful heart, you're not just giving to receive. You're giving from an infinite supply, honoring the Source of all provision, knowing His law is faithful.

4. Graciously Receive

We're taught from an early age how important it is to give. *Give your best. Give your tithes. Give to others.* But almost no one teaches us how to receive. In the law of giving and receiving, one cannot exist without the other. They're two sides of the same coin, two halves of the same breath. You inhale as naturally as you exhale. Both are required for life to flow.

If you struggle to give freely, it's often because you also struggle to receive. Somewhere along the way, you may have learned that receiving is selfish, indulgent, or undeserved. But that belief blocks the flow of abundance. To be abundant, you must be willing to receive it.

Remember our little apple tree? She doesn't reject the rain that the sky pours upon her. She graciously receives it, pulling it up into her roots. She never tells the soil not to share its nutrients. Instead, she receives them freely and uses them to produce her fruit.

When you receive money, love, kindness, or opportunity, you complete the sacred circuit of exchange. You allow the person who gave to you to participate in their own sacred exchange. There must always be a giver and a receiver to complete the circuit of abundance.

Receiving is active trust that you're worthy of the good coming your way, and what you graciously receive allows others to give freely.

Abundance is Your Birthright
Take time to reflect on the beliefs you inherited about

money from parents, religion, culture, or past experiences. Ask yourself: What messages did I absorb about money growing up? How have those beliefs shaped the way I earn, spend, or save? Which of those beliefs no longer serve me?

Then, consciously write a new story rooted in abundance. Declare that money is a resource meant to flow through you, not just to you.

Money isn't your enemy. It's not the root of evil. It's the energy of exchange that moves through life, creating opportunity and fostering community and connection. When you stop fearing it and start blessing it, you open the floodgates of possibility.

Abundance is your birthright, but it must first take root in your mind and heart before it shows up in your bank account. The more you align with the truth that God is your Source of infinite creative thought and ideas, the more freely money will flow.

You're not chasing money, you're aligning with abundance.

AFFIRMATION

"I am a conduit of infinite abundance. Money flows to me and through me with ease."

19

WHY WAS HE A RICH FOOL?

PRAYER

"Anchor me in Your infinite flow."

Parable of the Rich Fool

Jesus once told the story of a wealthy farmer whose fields produced an abundant harvest.

Overwhelmed by his success, the man said to himself, "I know what I'll do. I'll tear down my barns and build bigger ones to store all my grain and goods. Then I'll say to myself, 'You have plenty of good things laid up for many years. Take life easy. Eat, drink, and be merry.'"

But God said to him, "You fool! This very night, your life will be demanded from you. Then who will get what you have prepared for yourself?"

At first glance, it's easy to believe that the message Jesus was trying to tell us is that being rich is wrong. But when you take a closer look through the lens of true abundance, you can see that it wasn't his material possessions that were the problem, but his misunderstanding of them.

He was out of harmony with the spiritual principles that govern all life.

As we discussed previously, there are two ways to obtain material possessions. On the surface, they both appear to be abundant, but one is in harmony with divine expansion, while the other is material bloat.

True abundance isn't measured by possessions but by alignment with the abundant flow of Love itself.

This man wasn't foolish for expanding. He was foolish for believing his abundance was in his barns.

Why He Was a Rich Fool

1. He Believed Abundance Was External

The first mistake this man made was believing that abundance was something he could accumulate outside himself. He thought more barns and bigger harvests would bring him peace and satisfaction, but true abundance doesn't come from external wealth. It begins within.

Money, success, and status aren't abundant themselves. They're reflections of it, not the source of it.

Martin Luther King Jr., in his book, *Strength to Love*, said this man permitted the ends for which he lived to become confused with the means by which he lived.

The rich man believed the purpose of life was to store up

possessions, when the real purpose is to allow Love to expand through you.

"What does it profit a man to gain the whole world, yet lose his soul?" You can build barns full of grain and still starve spiritually. Without inner abundance, external wealth is meaningless.

2. He Blocked the Flow of Abundance

As we've covered, life must flow. Rivers flow, blood circulates, and air moves. Flow is the language of life. As soon as the flow is blocked, death or stagnation follows.

The rich fool stopped the flow. Instead of letting the abundant harvest move through him to continue expanding, he hoarded it for himself.

The law of abundance is that what you allow to flow through you multiplies. You must not only receive, but also give to complete the sacred exchange.

His wealth didn't make him foolish. It was his refusal to allow it to flow. He believed abundance was something to possess, not something to participate in.

3. He Forgot His Dependence

The fool said, "I'll tear down my barns and build bigger ones. I'll store my surplus grain."

He forgot who tilled the soil, who harvested the crops, who built the barns, and who baked the bread.

No one is truly self-made. Every success, every comfort, and every meal you eat is a collective effort of countless people.

From the farmer who plants the seed to the worker who harvests, to the grocer, the truck driver, and the cook, last night's dinner was a result of an intricate web of human cooperation.

The fool's blindness to this truth made him arrogant and alone. Gratitude would have grounded him and kept him connected.

But our dependence runs deeper still. We rely on others, but ultimately on the divine Source of all.

We welcome abundance through gratitude and alignment with Love's flow. The fool failed to see that every grain of wheat, every breath, and every heartbeat was a gift that he did not own. He trusted the barns instead of the Source. And when his time came, his barns were full, but his soul was empty.

True Abundance

We, too, face the same choice. Will we hoard what we have, convinced it's ours alone? Will we chase wealth outside ourselves and miss the infinite wellspring within? Will we block the flow, or will we become conduits through which abundance can multiply?

True abundance is never about how much you gather, but about how much you align with the infinite Supply within you and allow it to flow through you. It's about participating in the divine circulation of life, trusting that the more you give, the more you'll receive, ever expanding your capacity, ever increasing your harvest.

When you align with this flow and recognize your dependence on others, and on God, you stop living like a fool and start living like a co-creator, knowing that no matter how much or little you have, you always have access to the infinite Source.

You're not building bigger barns to store more possessions. You're building a sacred temple for the divine abundance to flow through you into the world around you.

AFFIRMATION

"I'm not the source. I'm the channel. Abundance flows to me and through me."

20

THE CHANNEL TO
RECEIVE ABUNDANCE

PRAYER

"May my heart remain open in gratitude so that abundance can flow freely through me."

The Practice of Gratitude

You've already seen that abundance is the natural rhythm of creation. Everything is always moving, always flowing, always expanding, but knowing abundance exists and actually experiencing it are two very different things. Many people live surrounded by abundance yet feel empty, disconnected, and deprived.

Why? Because abundance isn't something that forces its way into your life.

You must welcome it.

The way you receive abundance is through the practice of

gratitude. Gratitude aligns you with Love and opens the channel for the divine flow to move freely through you.

Imagine gratitude as turning on a lamp that's already plugged in. The electricity is already there, but nothing happens until you flip the switch.

Gratitude is the switch.

Gratitude is more than saying grace at dinner or thank you for gifts. Brené Brown says it isn't an attitude of gratitude, but a practice of gratitude. She says you never get in shape with a yoga attitude. You must practice yoga to see the benefits. You must intentionally practice gratitude to flip the switch on.

The practice of gratitude is more than simply appreciating what you have. It's aligning yourself with God's presence and opening yourself to receive the abundance already moving around you.

It's the inner knowing that *I am supported. I am safe. I am abundant because I am connected with God.*

True gratitude is your emotional response to the awareness of your constant connection to God. True gratitude transcends your experiences and possessions. It's the practice of detaching your gratitude from things, people, and experiences, and instead, attaching it to your ever present access to your Source. Recognizing God is with you, in you, and supplying you at every moment evokes the emotional humility of true gratitude.

As you practice this awareness, something beautiful happens. Gratitude begins to produce a deep joy, peace, and happiness that grounds you in every circumstance. It becomes easier to give thanks in all things.

From that place, gratitude is no longer something you try

to remember to include in your prayers. It becomes your natural posture.

How to Block Abundance

One of the fastest ways to block the abundant flow is through ungratefulness. It shows up in your thoughts, tone, attitude, and words. You can recognize it in the habits of negativity, complaining, criticizing, and chronic discontentment.

Ungratefulness can be subtle, and many people don't realize that they're blocking the very things they desire because of it. It rejects what you currently have because you want something different. It's the attitude *I don't want this.* Or, *this isn't enough.* Even when you don't say it out loud, your heart pushes away what Love gives you when you're consumed with negative thoughts about circumstances.

There's also a deep lack of trust in the Divine and His gifts. Maybe you don't realize it, but by rejecting them, you're saying, *You're wrong.* You're telling Him, *I know more than you.* When we don't trust the journey and His higher wisdom, we miss out on all the good and perfect gifts He has waiting for us.

When you hyper-focus on what's wrong, missing, or unexpected, you turn off the switch of abundance. When you say your circumstances are wrong or bad, when you complain about what Love has entrusted to you, the flow of abundance slows. Not because He withholds, but because you're not open to receive.

Gratitude, on the other hand, opens you up to receive,

knowing *I may not understand this, but I receive it. I honor it. I trust that this, too, is a good gift.*

Where ungratefulness pushes God's gifts away, gratitude pulls the gifts close, transforming 'what is' into 'enough.'

Dissatisfaction Isn't Ungratefulness

I want to clarify that there's a difference between ungratefulness and dissatisfaction. Both attitudes come from the natural desire for more. The difference is that ungratefulness rejects the current situation with complaint. Dissatisfaction accepts the current situation with gratitude, knowing it's a gift that prepares you for the greater things to come.

Ungratefulness avoids the undesired.

Dissatisfaction expands through it.

It's important not to squelch your natural dissatisfaction with the status quo, scarcity, and lack. But instead, with a heart of gratitude, move through this present moment with faith, knowing that no matter your situation, you're building something more.

Practice gratitude for your current situation, no matter how messy or mundane it is, and turn your heart toward what is possible, giving thanks for what is coming to you.

Your Words Reveal Your Heart

Gratitude begins in the mind, but it's expressed through the way you speak. Your words reveal the posture of your heart.

When your thoughts are rooted in fear and negativity, you'll express your lack of gratitude in little sighs of complaint, irritation over minor inconveniences, or negative talk about things you can't control, like the weather or traffic. These small habits may seem harmless, but they reinforce an inner narrative of ungratefulness.

Complaining closes the heart. Your focus is on what's wrong, what's missing, and what you wish were different.

Remember, what you give, you will receive. So pay attention to what words and attitude you're giving, because that's what you're going to receive more of.

Listen to what comes out of your mouth throughout the day. When you catch yourself complaining, pause, and without judgment, gently redirect your heart back to gratitude. Realign yourself with Love and your divine connection.

Through gratitude, traffic becomes a moment to breathe, rain becomes a reminder that the earth is nourished, and a delay is a time to slow down.

I'm not suggesting that you pretend everything is perfect. Instead, through the pain and mess, shift your inner posture from resistance to acceptance. Gratitude anchors you in the truth that everything, even the inconvenient and uncomfortable, can serve your growth and lead to goodness. You don't have to like it, but when you allow it to exist, you alleviate the additional pain and suffering that comes from fighting against it.

When you return your thoughts to the awareness that your breath, your life, and everything in it is intimately connected to God, gratitude naturally arises.

Give Thanks Before it Happens

One of the most powerful expressions of gratitude is to be

thankful before anything actually happens. This is gratitude in its highest form because it aligns you with what you cannot yet see. When you envision something coming into your life, like a restored relationship, a need fulfilled, or a dream taking shape, give thanks that it's already done before you have visual proof. Don't wait until after you see it.

Right before Jesus raised Lazarus from the dead, He prayed, "Father, I thank You that You have heard Me. I knew that You always hear Me."

He offered gratitude before the miracle.

He did this to express his appreciation for his continuous connection to the Father, and because he knew the miracle had already been done in the spirit world. That kind of gratitude isn't fantasy, but spiritual agreement with a higher reality. It tells the Father, *I trust Your ability, Your goodness, and Your timing. I trust that what You have started in the unseen realm, You'll finish in the visible realm.*

Gratitude in advance opens your heart to receive what God is preparing and aligns you with the unfolding long before you witness it.

Practical Practice of Gratitude

As a practical example of how this can work in your life, let's say you move into a small, rundown house because that's all you can afford. It's not what you want or like, but it's where you are.

If you're in the habit of unthankfulness, you focus on everything wrong. You'll notice the drafty windows and creaky floors. You'll complain about the cramped spaces and dingy walls because it's not what you hoped for. You'll live your days in frustration, discontentment, and resentment.

Now, when you shift into a state of gratitude, you begin in your present moment by recognizing that, even though you desire a nicer, bigger home, you have this one to keep your family warm, safe, and together. You intentionally ignore what's wrong and notice all that is right. You remind yourself that when it's the right time, you'll find a home that is more of what you desire.

Next, you shift into the spirit realm to create a vision for the house you desire to live in, remembering that it's the Father's great pleasure to give you the kingdom and to support you as you grow and expand. Envision all the details of your new home with extra space, fresh paint, and new windows.

To leave your vision open to the higher wisdom of Love, end your prayer with, "This or something better." Better meaning something better suited or better aligned that you just aren't aware of yet.

Finally, move through your days keeping yourself connected to Love, appreciating what you have, and thankful for what is coming. Cook yummy meals, decorate your walls, and play fun family games, never forgetting your connection to Love and the vision of your new home.

Over time, you may buy a new, bigger house or discover that your old home isn't cramped, but cozy, and with a new addition and a fresh remodel, your little home is everything you ever wanted.

Had you never opened yourself to gratitude, you would've spent your valuable days in frustration and discontentment.

You would've blocked the abundant flow, never receiving the good and perfect gifts available to you.

As you continue building the cathedral of your life, it will be your practice of gratitude that keeps the flow of abundance open and steady. Every time you give thanks, you align yourself with the Divine who is guiding you. You open the channel for resources you couldn't have planned and opportunities you couldn't have orchestrated.

Abundance will flow through you, reminding you to keep laying stones, one by one, until the vision within you becomes the life before you.

AFFIRMATION

"I welcome abundance with an open and grateful heart."

PART 6

DELAYS AND SETBACKS WILL HAPPEN

LIFE'S CHALLENGES

21

SETBACKS ARE PART
OF THE PROCESS

PRAYER

"When life doesn't go as I planned, may I trust that it is working for my good."

A 600 Year Delay

Construction of the Cologne Cathedral in Germany began in 1248 to be the tallest and most magnificent cathedral in the world. For over two hundred years, builders worked until financial troubles and shifted priorities brought everything to a standstill.

For more than 300 years, the unfinished structure stood frozen in time. But the dream never died. It wasn't until the 19th century, with renewed faith and determination, that builders returned to the site and picked up right where their ancestors had left off. After more than 600 years, Cologne Cathedral was finally completed in 1880.

Now, when people step into the breathtaking structure, they're unaware of the setback or the perseverance that went into its construction.

The setbacks and delays the builders went through weren't because they were failing or not on the right path. Setbacks are part of the actual process.

There will be chapters in life where progress slows, plans fall apart, doors close, or your energy is depleted. These moments don't mean you're off track. They don't mean your vision is wrong. They're the natural ebb and flow of life, and an important part of the work.

Setbacks Are Invitations

Since most delays and setbacks are painful and inconvenient, people have a natural response to despise them or feel defeated because of them, but setbacks aren't detours meant to derail you. These moments aren't punishments, but are opportunities to learn and grow. When disappointment, delay, and heartbreak knock at your door, they carry a sacred invitation to deepen your foundation, expand your capacity for Love, and tap into a strength you didn't know you had.

Pain has a way of bringing you to your knees, and though it feels like you're breaking, it's often the posture of transformation. When your life flips on its head, when the dream doesn't go as planned, or when someone you trusted betrays you, it's these moments that strip away illusion and awaken Love within. It's the bitter doorway through which the soul returns home.

The broken pieces of your heart that fall aren't wasted. They become the stained-glass windows, illuminating the world with the light within. Pain calls you inward, where the Divine waits with open arms, not to rescue you from the storm, but to ground you through it.

When you stop labeling setbacks as bad and start seeing them as necessary experiences, you realize they're not obstacles blocking your cathedral. Instead, every detour, delay, and disappointment is shaping you and preparing you for your greatest good.

A Holy Tempo

In the Invitation of this book, I talked about the slower pace of nature. Seeds do not rush to become trees. Rivers don't panic their way to the ocean. Flowers don't bloom instantly.

Nature moves with a holy tempo.

Because creation reflects its Creator, that tempo reveals God's tempo.

Rush, hurry, and panic aren't fruits of Love. They're symptoms of fear. When you feel a panicked urgency, needing immediate results, instant answers, or quick success, it's a sign you have slipped out of alignment.

Setbacks interrupt that frenzy.

They slow you down. It's frustrating when unexpected roadblocks halt you, but they also expose your faulty expectations.

In a world of instant downloads and same-day deliveries, we begin to expect immediate outcomes in every area of life. We want healing now. Growth now. Provision now. Clarity now.

Setbacks, as painful and disappointing as they can be,

often function as a reset. They pull you back to patience. They force you to reassess. They ask you to examine whether you're building in fear or in Love.

A setback can become a sacred pause.

A moment to ask: *Am I aligned? Am I building from peace or from panic? Am I striving, or am I trusting?*

Nature teaches us this pattern again and again: Love is patient.

Setbacks Come In Different Forms

Setbacks come in many forms, each refining you in different ways.

Some are self-inflicted, caused by your own choices, mistakes, or self-destructive lifestyle. These are the times you procrastinate, sabotage your progress, or make decisions you later regret.

Other setbacks are caused by people around you, like betrayal, broken promises, or rejection, which leave you hurt and questioning your path.

There are also circumstantial setbacks beyond your control, such as illness, job loss, or global events that upend your life.

Setbacks don't arrive neatly packaged with navigation steps. They come as unexpected blows, leaving you disoriented and unsure of what to do next. They shake your confidence, blur your vision, and make the earth below you feel unstable.

When the invitation comes dressed as loss or pain, say 'yes' to the sacred classroom of your own awakening, for it's here, in the dark night of the soul, that you meet Love in his holy temple.

When you're in the middle of a setback, it's tempting to spiral into self-pity and despair. Instead, open yourself up to what you're meant to learn through it. Pause and ask:

What is this teaching me?

What is this revealing about where I need to grow?

How might this be redirecting me toward something even better?

Do I trust that this is working for my greatest good, even though I can't see how?

Stop seeing setbacks as punishments and start viewing them as sacred opportunities for growth. They aren't the end of your story. They're part of the story that makes your cathedral worth building.

The most beautiful parts of your life often come from what you once called a setback. The heartbreak that forced you to grow. The disappointment that taught you perseverance. The closed door that redirected you to a better one.

Life is never a straight line from beginning to end. Every great journey includes chapters of waiting, sorrow, and redirection. Without them, you'd never develop the depth of character needed to sustain your vision.

AFFIRMATION

"Setbacks are my teacher. I am a willing student."

22

FAILURE DOESN'T EXIST

PRAYER

"Help me see every misstep as a stepping stone. Remind me that my past mistakes don't define my worth."

The Fear of Failure

Most people never lift a single hammer because they're afraid of failing. They spend years dreaming, planning, preparing, but never actually building. And if they do find the courage to start, many abandon their efforts the moment things don't go as planned. One mistake, one setback, and they convince themselves it's over.

I know this deeply because I've lived it many times.

Several years ago, Matt and I walked through one of the hardest seasons in our business. Everything we had worked for seemed to crumble overnight because of a few business decisions we made. What started as one step forward suddenly became a hundred steps back. It was painful and humiliating.

I remember lying under the covers one evening, tears soaking my pillow, convinced I had failed.

When Matt came home, he asked, "What are you doing?"

Through tears, I said, "Trying not to quit."

It wasn't life I wanted to give up on, but my dream. I had read a quote earlier that day, "It's only failure if you quit." In that moment, quitting felt easier than continuing.

After my pity party was over, I decided not to give up. What I thought was the end turned out to be more like a pivot point I didn't know we needed, because less than a year later, COVID hit. Had we not gone through our setback, we wouldn't have been prepared for the hardship of the pandemic.

Looking back at that experience made me realize that failure isn't real. Instead, it's the label we give our painful missteps. Somewhere along the way, we were taught to see our mistakes as signs that we're not good enough or cut out for the job. But in reality, though painful, they're simply feedback on where we need to grow.

Failure Doesn't Exist

The belief that falling is failure isn't natural. It's learned. Think back when you first learned to walk. How many times did you fall? Hundreds? And not once did anyone shame you for falling.

No one said, "You're a failure because you can't walk yet."

They clapped, cheered, and celebrated every time you tumbled, because they knew you were that much closer.

Falling is part of the process. Mistakes are part of mastery. The only true failure is giving up.

Unfortunately, as we grow, society teaches us something different. In school, you only get so many chances to spell a word correctly before you get the red stamp: FAILED. Forgot the formula? F. Answered a question wrong? F.

From that moment on, we start to internalize the belief that mistakes define us and that imperfections equal worthlessness. But life isn't a classroom.

No cosmic teacher is handing out grades, because even God knows our frame and remembers that we are dust. He's not standing over us with a ruler measuring our perfection. No, he knows we're toddlers stumbling around this planet learning how to walk.

Life offers countless second chances and constant opportunities to try again. As long as you're still breathing, you're not failing. You're learning.

Every stumble is feedback. Every setback is information. Every mistake is simply a data point pointing you toward a better way forward. Use the data to grow and learn.

Edison understood this when he said of the lightbulb, "I have not failed. I've just found 10,000 ways that won't work."

Each attempt refined his process, and each disappointment got him one step closer to his final success.

What you call failure today may be the very thing that prepares you for what's next. It's the storm that tests your foundation. It's the teacher who equips you.

Shame is Your Teacher

In Chapter 12, we discussed how shame attacks your identity. If you notice you're feeling shame after making a mistake, pay attention, because it's pointing you to a faulty belief about your identity.

Pushing others away with defensiveness when receiving feedback or arguing to prove you're right are signs that you're feeling shame. Signals of shame are withdrawing from life, wanting to avoid others, or pulling away from relationships. Harsh self-criticism or loss of motivation are other signs of your shame.

When shame is your response to mistakes or shortcomings, you may not recognize it, but you believe that your identity is linked to your actions. Meaning what you do and what you create is an extension of you. So if someone rejects your idea, they're rejecting you. If someone criticizes your work, they're criticizing you.

When your worth is directly linked to your output, then there's no room for mistakes. You must get it right every time to be good enough. This leads to perfectionism.

Don't judge your shame too harshly. Instead, let shame be your teacher. Shame is showing you where you have a faulty subconscious belief. It's alerting you where you have work to do.

Reprogram Your Mind

Once you recognize a faulty belief, your goal is to stop the shame spiral and reprogram your mind. Thank shame for doing its job in revealing the lie you believed. Awareness is the first step toward change.

Now, it's time to begin replacing that belief.

One effective way to reprogram your subconscious mind is through a practice called auto-suggestion. Most of the time, your subconscious mind runs quietly in the background, sending your beliefs up into your conscious thoughts. But you're not powerless in that process. With intention and repetition, you can begin impressing new messages into your subconscious.

This doesn't happen overnight. The subconscious mind learns through consistent repetition and emotional conviction. The more often you repeat a new belief, the more familiar it becomes, and over time, your mind begins to accept it as truth.

Here is a simple way to practice auto-suggestion:

1. Identify the False Belief

Start by clearly naming the belief shame exposed.

It may sound like:

"I'm not good enough."
"If I make a mistake, people will reject me."
"My value depends on my performance."

Bringing the belief into the light weakens its hold.

2. Replace It With Truth

Now create a new statement that reflects the truth you want your mind to accept.

For example:

"My mistakes do not define my worth."
"I am learning and growing every day."
"My value is inherent, not earned."

Choose words that feel both empowering and believable.

3. Repeat It Daily

The subconscious mind learns through repetition. Speak your new belief out loud each day. Write it in your journal. Repeat it when old thoughts resurface.

You're not trying to force yourself to believe it immediately. You're planting a new seed in your mind.

4. Add Emotion and Visualization

The subconscious responds strongly to emotion and imagery. As you repeat the new belief, picture yourself living from it. Imagine how you would think, speak, and act if it were already true. Feel yourself believing it.

The more vividly you experience it in your mind, the more deeply the message sinks in.

5. Be Patient With the Process

Your current beliefs were formed through years of repetition and experience. Reprogramming your mind takes time, but every time you choose truth over shame, you weaken the old pattern and strengthen the new one.

Little by little, your inner dialogue begins to change. The voice that once condemned you becomes a voice that encourages you. The faulty belief that once lived quietly in the shadows is replaced with a new truth about who you really are.

Missteps are always going to bruise your ego. No one likes making mistakes, but it doesn't need to define you or derail your entire building project.

Remember, you're a cosmic toddler learning how to walk, and even if you've fallen into the ditch, it's never too late to get back up, learn, and begin again.

Each time you choose to get up after falling, you're succeeding. So, stand up and dust yourself off. Rip up the report card, and take that next step, however small, in the direction of the life calling you forward.

The masterpiece is still being built, and you're still its builder.

AFFIRMATION

"When I fall seven times, I will get up eight."

23

ARE YOU SELF-SABOTAGING?

PRAYER

"Give me the courage to face myself. Help me to see clearly where fear controls what I do."

Your Biggest Obstacle

Roadblocks and setbacks are inevitable. They're part of living a human life. Every person who's ever dared to create something beautiful has come face to face with financial setbacks, missed opportunities, broken relationships, or simply seasons when nothing seems to move forward.

On the surface, these difficult circumstances appear to be the reason you can't build your cathedral. It seems like the economy, your spouse, your job, or the lack of money is what's preventing you from achieving your best life. But the real obstacle isn't outside of you. It's within you.

Circumstances may get in your way, block the path you're

on, or stall your progress, but they cannot prevent you from doing your divine purpose to expand in Love.

It's not your circumstances, your past, or the people around you who force you to bury your talent in the earth. It's you.

You're the one who decides to stop, to give up, and abandon your cathedral. This is what is called self-sabotage, and it's destroyed more dreams than any external circumstance ever could.

In *The War of Art*, Steven Pressfield names this invisible enemy Resistance. He writes,

"Resistance seems to come from outside ourselves. We locate it in spouses, jobs, bosses, kids…[but] Resistance arises from within. It is self-generated and self-perpetuated. Resistance is the enemy within."

Resistance isn't isolated to the weak or the undisciplined. It's the human condition that's plagued us from the dawn of time. We have always been our own biggest enemy.

It's a bitter pill to face the reality that you're the one blocking your abundant life. But once you recognize that self-sabotage is an internal force, not an external enemy, you reclaim your power. If Resistance comes from within you, then so does the power to overcome it.

When you stop blaming the world and start taking radical ownership of your thoughts, your habits, and your choices, you change your life. You stop reacting to life and start creating it.

Nothing can stop a person who realizes they're both the problem and the solution.

Fear is at the Core

At the root of self-sabotage isn't laziness, weakness, or lack of discipline. It's fear.

Fear itself isn't the enemy. In fact, you need fear, because its job is to keep you alive. It's fear that stops you from stepping into oncoming traffic or walking too close to a cliff's edge.

But when you put fear on the throne of your life, it stops protecting you and starts imprisoning you. It will see danger everywhere, like in new opportunities, unfamiliar faces, and the vulnerability of connection.

Fear whispers, *Stay where it's safe.*

So, you hold back. You hesitate. You talk yourself out of trying.

It's not that you don't want to succeed. It's that success itself feels too risky. Change feels threatening, and growth feels unsafe. The very things that could expand your life, fear makes you believe are dangerous.

Fear has many disguises. It shows up as overthinking, perfectionism, avoidance, defensiveness, or control. Sometimes fear wears lies like *you're not ready.* Or *you're not capable.* Or *you're not enough.* Other times, it dresses up as logic, convincing you to wait until the timing is perfect or until you feel more confident.

Here are some ways fear speaks to you:

Fear of failure: "What if I give everything I've got and I still can't do it?"

Fear of success: "What if I achieve this and can't keep it up? What if people expect more than what I'm capable of?"

Fear of judgment: "What if people think I'm a fraud?"

Fear of rejection: "What if I put myself out there, and they tell me no?"

Fear of change: "Who will I be if I'm no longer the person I've always been?"

When you water the seeds of fear by letting them grow in your thoughts, you give fear control over your life. Fear will be your master, deciding what you try, what you risk, and how small you'll stay.

It will demand that you bury your talent.

Awareness is the Key

The moment you begin to see fear running your life and how you're standing in your own way, you reclaim your power. Awareness is the first difficult step, but the most transformative. Once you name Resistance, you can no longer hide behind it. Once you see how fear has been running the show, you can take control back.

You'll never eliminate fear. It'll always be part of your journey, and you'll always have an inner critic that tries to keep you small. But awareness gives you the upper hand, reminding you that while fear may always be present, it doesn't have to be in charge.

Awareness is powerful, but transformation requires you to return again and again to the kingdom of God within you, where you rewrite the stories that have held you back.

Beat Resistance

Getting out of your own way isn't a one-time break-through. You're not going to wake up one morning and never self-sabotage your building progress. As we've already established, this is a lifelong commitment to the daily renewal of your mind.

Give yourself lots and lots of grace. It's one of the most difficult journeys to live in the tension between the spirit realm and the physical world. It's a narrow path that very few people find, because it's not easy to deny your ego and live from the Spirit.

Notice when shame comes knocking on your door, attempting to make Resistance part of your identity. Don't be afraid of shame. He's trying to show you where you need to grow, but let him in. Keep your gate firmly locked, reminding him that you're human, learning how to shed limitations and expand in Love.

You don't overcome Resistance by brute force or sheer willpower, but by going inward, aligning your thoughts with divine reality rather than fear-based illusions. It's committing to the daily work of thought stopping and intentional auto-suggestion. It's taking control of the garden of your mind, so the little foxes can't destroy it.

Over time, your daily practice will reprogram your subconscious, beating Resistance and transforming your life.

AFFIRMATION

"I have the power to get out of my own way."

24

SEASONS OF BUILDING

PRAYER

"Help me welcome each season as sacred, by walking faithfully with Love as my guide."

Time for Everything

Throughout this book, we've returned again and again to the wisdom of nature. Nature quietly reveals how life works and how the Divine moves.

In nature, nothing rushes and nothing resists the rhythms it was given. The earth faithfully moves through its seasons.

We often assume growth should be linear. We think we should always be moving forward, always expanding, always building upward. But real growth doesn't work that way. Just like the natural world, our lives move in cycles. There are seasons of planting and seasons of harvest, seasons of movement and seasons of stillness.

There's a time for everything.

Every season has a purpose, preparing you for the next. The planting teaches endurance. The waiting builds patience. The harvest reveals fulfillment of co-creation.

Life's seasons rarely follow neat timelines. They don't arrive on schedule, and they don't all last the same length of time. A season of joy may stretch for years. A season of waiting may linger longer than you hoped.

But no matter how long they stay, seasons always change.

Learning how to move through the seasons without resistance is an important skill you can develop as you build.

The Four Seasons of Building

Let's look at how the four seasons mirror the building of your cathedral:

Spring: New Beginnings

Spring is the season of birth and renewal. It's the time when new ideas blossom and opportunities emerge. This is when the vision awakens, energy expands, and ideas spark.

Seeds you planted long ago finally break through the surface. The air is alive with potential.

To lean into this season, embrace its spirit of curiosity and newness. Focus on the creative process rather than outcomes, and give your ideas the space and time they need to take form. Nurture yourself, trusting that what you create now is part of something bigger.

Summer: Growth, Work, and Joy

Summer is the season of focused building. The work shifts from planning to doing. You're no longer sketching blueprints or imagining what might be. You're typing the words, folding the laundry, or putting in long hours. Consistent, sustained action is key here. The habits you develop and the daily steps you take all become the scaffolding that supports your larger vision.

The energy of this season is high, steady, and purposeful. Just as a summer garden requires daily watering, pruning, and care, your goals demand regular attention. Growth happens rapidly now, but only if you stay present and engaged with the work in front of you. It's the season of steady progress, one deliberate action after another.

To lean into summer's rhythm, commit to showing up every single day, even when motivation fades, and the work feels mundane. At the same time, be mindful of your pace, as excessive pushing without rest can lead to burnout. Create space to recharge, knowing that sustained effort is more effective than frantic striving.

This is the grit season. Keep your eyes turned toward the rising cathedral, not just the brick in your hand.

Autumn: Reflection and Release

Autumn is the season of harvest and reflection. It's a sacred pause to bring your awareness back to what you've built so far. The walls are rising, and the scaffolding stretches high, but before laying the next stone, it's time to evaluate. What's thriving? Where does the structure feel strong? What do I need to release before the next phase begins?

Use this slower season to prune away habits or distractions that no longer serve you. Give your days space for gratitude and evaluation. Pause to ensure your next steps align with the cathedral you're creating.

The energy of this time slows and becomes reflective. Be careful not to force yourself to race ahead or push harder. Instead, practice thoughtful realignment of your values.

To lean into this season, practice releasing. Let go of habits, routines, or beliefs that once served you but no longer do.

Just as trees let go of the leaves that once served them well, trust that releasing is not loss but preparation. It's a proactive decision to make space for more in the future.

Winter: Rest and Restoration

Winter is often the most misunderstood and challenging season. The cold, bitter winds of life can feel like abandonment and isolation. The chill settles in, and visible progress halts.

But beneath the stillness, an essential part of the process begins — rest. The foundation settles, and the walls set in as the structure fortifies. In nature, the roots force themselves deeper into the earth, strengthening the tree.

Winter's energy is stillness, a slowing down to rest.

To lean into winter, draw yourself into your inner world. Allow your mind, body, and spirit to recover from the labor of building. This is a time to deepen your connection with Love through prayer, meditation, silence, and self-care. It's okay to close your calendar, cancel plans, and go inward.

Though it seems like nothing is happening, this is sacred preparation. Without winter's stillness, the next spring's growth would be shallow and short-lived. When you honor winter, your cathedral strengthens from within.

Seasons Are the Sacred Rhythm of Life

Some seasons will feel exhilarating, and others will feel heavy. Some will stretch you beyond what you think you can handle. Others will bring such peace that you'll never want them to end.

All are holy.

Allow each season to emerge in its time. They're the sacred rhythm of life. Don't try to cling to summer when autumn is calling you to release. Don't wish for spring when winter is inviting you inward. Don't long for the harvest when new seeds are waiting to be planted.

Welcome the gifts each season brings.

AFFIRMATION

"Each season is working for my good and preparing me for what's next."

25

———————

ALL IS GOOD!

PRAYER

"When life feels messy or confusing, remind me that even this moment is working for me, not against me."

The Good and the Bad

Life is full of moments we quickly label as good or bad. It's human nature to try to make sense of what happens to us, so we create an inner grading system for our experiences. We assume that if we can collect enough good moments and avoid the bad ones, we will finally arrive at happiness.

So we sort life accordingly.

Experiences that feel pleasant, go our way, and fit our expectations are labeled good. The ones that hurt, disrupt our plans, or challenge our worldview are labeled bad. We celebrate when it works out and despair when it doesn't.

There's a problem with this grading system. Our perspective is incredibly limited.

We can only see a single moment at a time, one snapshot of a much larger story. We don't know what the next moment will bring or how today's experience might weave itself into the larger design of our lives.

What feels like a setback today may become the very thing that propels you forward tomorrow. What looks like a blessing today may later reveal itself as a detour. Yet we judge our lives as if the present moment is the whole story.

We say losing a job is bad. Getting promoted is good. A breakup is bad. A new relationship is good. But how many times have you looked back and realized that what once felt like a disaster turned out to be a hidden gift? And how many moments you once celebrated later became a burden you wished you had never picked up?

We can't see the full picture while we're living inside it. We see only the moment in front of us, unaware of how each experience is quietly shaping the path ahead.

The Old Man Who Lost His Horse

This ancient Chinese parable beautifully illustrates this truth:

> "Once upon a time, a farmer's horse ran away.
> His neighbors said, "We're so sorry. What terrible luck."
> The farmer simply replied, "Maybe."

The next day, the horse returned with seven wild horses.

"Wow! What great fortune!" the neighbors said.

"Maybe," the farmer replied.

The following day, the farmer's son tried to tame one of the horses and broke his leg.

"Oh no! That's awful!" the neighbors said.

"Maybe," the farmer answered.

The next day, soldiers came to conscript young men into the army, but they passed over the farmer's son because of his broken leg.

"What wonderful news!" the neighbors said.

"Maybe," the farmer said once more." (Huainan zi, ca. 139 BCE)

We don't know our entire timeline. What appears bad today may lead to something good tomorrow.

To live with unwavering peace, rather than riding an emotional rollercoaster based on good and bad circumstances, you must abandon your inner grading scale and adopt the practice of radical acceptance. Allow every life experience to come without judgment, trusting that Love is weaving every thread into His perfect will.

Radical Acceptance

People struggle with the concept of acceptance because they confuse it with approval. They feel that if they accept something they don't like or agree with, they're putting their stamp of approval on it. Acceptance feels like you're saying, *I'm ok with this.* Or, *I'm happy this is happening.*

Acceptance doesn't mean approval at all. Acceptance means allowing what is to take up space in your life without resistance. You don't put energy into trying to reject it or change it. You stop fighting it and allow it to be.

Practicing radical acceptance means living a life of total surrender to what shows up each day. When sickness, an unexpected bill, or a flat tire sucker punches you, instead of resisting it with anger and frustration, you take a deep breath and allow the experience to be part of your life. You accept the divine gift with complete trust that God is working for you.

This isn't toxic positivity or pretending you're ok with the situation. You meet each moment surrendering to the unknown wisdom of Love, maintaining a peace that no matter what, you're supported and will find your way through it.

Focus on the Solution

When challenges arise, the mind's instinct is to fixate on the problem by replaying what went wrong, spiraling into despair, and imagining worst-case scenarios. But that pattern keeps you stuck in fear, disconnecting you from Love and making matters worse.

There's always a way of escape, even if you can't see it yet. Norman Vincent Peale wrote, "Every problem has in it the seeds of its own solution." Every problem has a solution. You just have to look for it.

Instead of focusing on what's wrong, practice shifting your attention to what's possible. Live in a state of curiosity, always looking for the answer instead of fixating on the problem.

When you choose to look for the next right step instead of rehearsing the pain, you move from reaction to creation, from fear to Love. You activate your power of imagination to create solutions, find answers, and build with intention.

Understanding Your Problems

Before you can move toward a solution, it helps to understand the kind of problem you're facing. Not every challenge in life is the same, and confusion about this is often what keeps people feeling stuck.

Problems fit into one of three categories.

1. Problems you can solve.

The majority of problems fall under this category. These will be problems like learning a new skill, improving your health, or changing a flat tire. These are challenges that require effort, creativity, learning, or persistence. You may not know the answer yet, but a path forward exists. It might require gaining new knowledge, asking for help, or trying a different strategy.

When you face this type of problem, your role is to be curious and resourceful, looking for the next best step.

2. Problems you can't solve.

Some problems cannot be solved because they were never problems to begin with. Marie Forleo explains in her book, *Everything is Figureoutable*, if something truly isn't figureoutable, then it isn't a problem. It's a fact of life.

Loss, aging, and other people's choices fall into this category. You can't undo circumstances, stop time, or control another person's actions. When we treat these realities as problems to solve, we exhaust ourselves fighting a losing battle.

The way forward is radical acceptance.

Remember, acceptance doesn't mean you approve of what happened. It means you stop resisting reality and begin reframing your thoughts, your responses, and your perspective so you can find a path forward with peace and clarity.

3. Problems that need a decision.

Sometimes we face problems that feel impossible to solve, but it's not the solution that is lacking. It's your fortitude to make a decision that's lacking. Fear is usually the reason why you'll stand immobile at a crossroad of indecision. You remain stuck, hoping the situation will eventually resolve itself, but instead, it leaves you spiraling in confusion.

To move forward in these situations is to practice reframing your mind from fear to trust. Trust that you, connected to the mind of Love, can make decisions, and if you make the wrong one, you'll be able to learn from it and then make the next right step.

Anytime you're met with a problem, pause, breathe, and bring yourself back into the present moment.

Remind yourself, *in this moment, I'm safe. Love is guiding me.*

You aren't abandoned in your circumstances. You're being led through them. The Divine is never absent. He's always whispering solutions, ideas, and new paths in the quiet of your own heart.

You figured life out up till this point, and you'll continue to figure it out.

All Is Working for Your Good

When you stop judging life by its appearances and begin to practice looking with your spiritual eyes, you tap into your inner knowing that something larger is at work, even when you can't yet see the evidence.

You may not understand the purpose right away. In fact, you rarely do. When you're in the middle of heartache, confusion, or loss, everything feels senseless and unfair. You can't yet see how everything will fit together, because you're still standing in the broken pieces.

But one day after the dust settles and the ache softens, you'll look back and see clearly. You'll realize that even the pain and struggle were part of the design. The lessons that once felt cruel will reveal themselves as sacred teachers. The very moments that broke you open were the ones that transformed you.

You don't need to know the purpose to trust that there is one. In time, when you turn around and see where Love has led you, you'll realize that nothing is wasted. You can rest knowing that even this has a purpose and is working for you.

Every experience is part of the construction of your cathedral. Radical acceptance will give you the strength to walk through each day with a peace that passes understanding.

All of life, with its ups and downs, mountains and valleys, storms and sunshine, is working together for your good.

AFFIRMATION

"Everything is working together for my highest good. Even when I cannot see the purpose, I trust the process."

PART 7

BUILT TO LAST

PERSONAL INTEGRITY

26

INTENTION OVER ACHIEVEMENT

PRAYER

"Support me as I become the person You designed me to be."

Goals Without Intention

Most people, when they get a vision for their lives, rush straight into setting goals. They write long to-do lists, habits to start, and milestones to reach. And while goals can be powerful motivators, starting here often leads to frustration.

Goals without intention are like laying stones without mortar. They may look strong for a while, but they won't hold under pressure. You might make progress for a few days or weeks, but as soon as life gets hard, motivation crumbles.

Without the deeper why that intention provides, goals become chores, and progress turns into striving. This is why so many people find themselves trapped in the exhausting cycle of starting and stopping. They begin with excitement, fueled by willpower, but when results don't come fast enough, they lose momentum.

Then the shame sets in, *I'm such a failure.* So they try harder next time with more goals and more pressure, or they give up altogether. And the cycle repeats.

Intention is the mortar that holds your progress together. Without it, even the most beautiful plan eventually falls apart.

The Subtle Trap of Goals

Goals have their place. They give direction and motivation, but the subtle trap is that they can convince you that your life isn't enough until you achieve them.

It's the "I'll be happy when…" lie.

I'll be happy when I lose 20 pounds.

I'll feel secure when I have $1,000 in the bank.

I'll feel worthy when I publish the book.

This kind of thinking keeps joy just out of reach, always chasing, but never arriving. No matter how much you accomplish, the horizon keeps moving. You reach one goal only to find another waiting in the distance.

When your happiness depends on achievement, you'll never get it, because progress never ends.

Goals are wonderful servants but terrible masters. They're meant to guide your energy, not define your worth.

Goals with Intention

Before you list what you'd like to achieve, you must root

yourself in the present moment. You must learn to embody the state of being you desire now, not after you achieve.

That means claiming your happiness and worth in this moment before the book is written, before the debt is paid, before the weight is lost. It's the belief that *my happiness isn't defined by how much weight I lose. I choose to be happy and beautiful now as I care for my body.*

To embody your desired state in the present is to live with intention. Intention is the deeper why beneath the what. It's the inner alignment that keeps you steady when results are slow and the path uncertain.

Without intention, goals demand perfection. With intention, goals become expressions of your deepest values.

You begin to live from a space of being rather than from a space of achievement. You begin to define yourself by who you are as you achieve, rather than by what you achieve.

Goals and intentions aren't enemies. They're partners. They just need to work in the right order.

Intentions are *how* you live: your state of being and who you choose to be in each moment.
Goals are *what* you achieve: the milestones, outcomes, and results you can measure.

A goal says, "I'm going to run a half-marathon."
An intention says, "I commit to showing up for myself with discipline and joy."

A goal says, "I'm going to make an extra thousand dollars this year."

An intention says, "I choose to embody abundance and generosity in all that I do."

A goal says, "We'll go on one date a week to strengthen our marriage."
An intention says, "I will show up as a loving partner."

Goals live in the future.
Intentions live right now.
Goals are about doing.
Intentions are about being.

Live in the Present

When you live only for our goals, you'll constantly live in the future, chasing what you haven't yet obtained. And in doing so, you miss the only moment that exists — the present moment.

Right now is the only moment you have to build. Yesterday is gone and can't be changed, tomorrow hasn't happened yet, and is uncertain, but now is here. Now is all you've got.

Living with intention frees you from the weight of what's behind you and the anxiety of what's ahead. When you root yourself in the present, something sacred shifts. You stop postponing happiness until you reach a goal. You stop waiting for perfect conditions to feel peace. You begin to see that joy and contentment aren't rewards, but choices available to you now.

Don't stop setting goals or working to grow, just be careful not to place your worth in what you achieve.

Goals without intention are empty. They can give you

accomplishments, but rarely deliver peace. When intention leads, even the smallest steps become sacred.

Begin to measure your life not by what you build, but by who you become as you build it.

AFFIRMATION

"I am grounded in who I am, not what I achieve."

27

BE GREAT IN SMALL THINGS

PRAYER

"Let every small act be a reflection of Love within me."

Greatness Isn't In the Grand

We often confuse greatness with what is grand and visible. We think people are great because of their titles, wealth, or influence. We measure greatness by the size of the platform or the applause it draws.

True greatness is found in the areas of your life that others can't see.

A cathedral's magnificence lies in the strength of its foundation and the quality of its materials. Its greatness is found in the hidden places.

Society celebrates the visible achievements like promotions, milestones, and recognition, but those are simply the outcomes of what you've built in private. Greatness is cultivated in the small, consistent acts of integrity, in the choices you make when no one is watching.

Greatness Starts at Home

Nowhere does this truth matter more than at home.

It's easy to show kindness, patience, and respect in public, where reputation is on the line, but it's in your closest relationships that your true character is revealed.

Familiarity often breeds contempt, and many people unconsciously save their best selves for strangers and offer their family only the scraps of what's left over. They give their smiles to the world and their frustration to the ones who love them most.

The measure of a person's greatness isn't how you treat the world, but how you treat your own household. Practicing kindness in the small, daily ways with your spouse, your children, your parents, and your friends is the truest form of greatness.

You cultivate greatness daily through the small, intentional choices you make in your relationships. Think of the following practices as the hidden mortar of your foundation, small but essential to the strength of what you're building.

1. Give Unconditional Respect

Give unconditional respect, first to yourself, then to others, because at a fundamental level every human is a sacred temple and deserves to be treated as such, even if they don't yet know it.

It's easy to be respectful when others are kind, but true integrity is choosing respect even when others are rude, ungrateful, or dismissive.

Living with integrity means acting from who you are, not reacting to how others behave. It's remembering that your tone, words, and attitude can build or destroy a connection.

When you choose unconditional respect, you're saying, "I won't let your behavior determine mine."

Respect begins inward. It's how you speak to yourself, how you handle your mistakes, how you regard your reflection in the mirror. From that well of self-respect flows how you treat others, and what you give, you will receive.

2. Let Your Yes Be Yes, and Your No Be No

Another way to build integrity into your cathedral is to let your words mean what they say.

How many times have you agreed to something you didn't want to do? Maybe you said yes out of obligation, fear of disappointing someone, or because you didn't want to appear selfish.

Saying yes when your heart says no is self-betrayal, and self-betrayal is one of the most corrosive forces to the soul. It creates resentment, exhaustion, and quiet anger that seeps into everything you build.

Integrity begins with honesty, not just with others, but with yourself. When you honor your authentic 'no,' you build a structure rooted in truth. And when you give a whole-hearted 'yes,' it carries the full weight of your presence and commitment.

Your structure can't be shaken when rooted in truth.

3. Keep Your Word

When you make a commitment, it's important to keep it. Integrity with others is built when they know they can depend on you to do what you promised.

It's easy to back out when you're tired or disinterested, but each broken promise chips away at the trust in your relationships and weakens your own self-respect.

Take your time before verbally committing to something with your spouse, children, or friends. Make sure that you're aligned with your yes or no. Take time to get clarity, so that you're not making a rash commitment that you'll later regret.

Once you say yes, follow through with a good attitude and a willing heart.

This doesn't mean you should never cancel plans, because we know life happens, but make cancellations the exception, not the rule.

Give clear answers and stand by them. It tells others and yourself that you're reliable and can be trusted.

4. Let Your No Be Enough

Another practice of greatness in the small things is to let your 'no' be enough. This practice sounds simple, but it challenges many of us because we were taught that no is a bad word.

As we know, it's impossible to say yes to all things all the time. For every yes, you must say no to something else. No isn't a bad word. It's a necessary part of expanding in Love. Welcome no into your vocabulary as a valuable word to use with confidence.

When you say no, let that be enough. Notice your urge to over-explain or justify it when you decline an invitation. This urge is usually an act of people-pleasing, which comes from your fear of disappointing someone, being misunderstood, being rejected, or causing conflict. But every time you over-explain, you subtly weaken your integrity.

When you say no, you don't owe anyone an explanation. A simple, gracious response is enough.

"Thank you for thinking of me, but I won't be able to make it."

"I appreciate the offer, but that doesn't work for me right now."

No more, no less.

Your worth isn't dependent on others' approval. Your boundaries don't need permission.

Letting your no be enough builds self-trust. It reminds you that you're safe to stand in truth without apology.

5. Say Exactly What You Need

Be honest about what you need or desire. Most people struggle with the vulnerability of asking for something, so they hide their true feelings by hinting, minimizing, suppressing, or hoping others will just know.

This avoidance is a subtle form of dishonesty, and over time, erodes both your integrity and your relationships.

When you don't voice your needs or expectations by denying or lying about them, you betray yourself. This kind of betrayal shows up in subtle lies.

You say, "It's fine," when it's not.
You say, "I don't care," when you do.
You pretend you're okay when you're drowning.

You may think you're protecting yourself, but you're really eroding your spirit and disconnecting from others. Each time you silence the truth, you build walls of resentment, misunderstanding, and disconnection.

It's easy to become frustrated with someone when they don't meet your needs, but many times their failure isn't because they denied you, but because they didn't know your unspoken expectations. You may quietly hope the other person will know what you need, somehow reading your mind or picking up on subtle hints. When they don't respond the way you hoped, disappointment quickly turns into irritation or resentment. People can't meet the expectations you never told them about. Expecting others to interpret your unspoken desires will always lead to frustration.

When you express what you're feeling or what you hope for, you give the other person the opportunity to understand you rather than unknowingly fall short of a standard they never knew existed.

Learning to voice your needs clearly and calmly isn't selfish. It's foundational to the law of giving and receiving. You're voicing what you'd like to receive, removing the guessing game, and giving the other person an opportunity to give. It's essential for healthy relationships and for living with authenticity.

It takes courage to express what you need without knowing how others will respond. But their reaction isn't your responsibility. Your responsibility is to speak with honesty and

Love. Most people would rather know what you really need than try to guess and get it wrong.

Try small, simple truths:

"Can you help me pick up the house?"
"I'm hurt and need to talk about what happened."
"Can you watch the kids so I can have some quiet
time to recharge?"

Honest communication strengthens your inner foundation and builds deeper trust with others.

The Small Moments are Sacred

The greatness of your life isn't measured by grand, headline-worthy moments. It's the small, private ones.

It's in how you speak when you're tired.

How you treat your family when no one is watching.

How do you practice patience in the mundane?

Be faithful with the small bricks, and the cathedral will take care of itself.

One day, the people who know you best will testify to the life you built. Your children will be the ones to rise and call you blessed. Your husband will be the one to honor you as his jeweled crown. The ones you love will carry your kindness as part of their own story.

Don't despise the small moments. They're the sacred mortar of your legacy, the building blocks of your cathedral. Every act of kindness, every gentle word, every choice to Love is forming something eternal.

One day, you'll look back and see that you built something great, one small, holy act at a time.

AFFIRMATION

"I am faithful in the small things. Every action I take builds the life I desire."

28

RETURN TO LOVE

PRAYER

"Guide me back home when I lose my way."

It's Human to Forget

Even after everything we've covered about finding meaning and purpose in life, being human is still one of the strangest experiences imaginable.

We arrive here without memory of where we came from, and when we die, we step into a mystery we can't comprehend. In between those two unknowns, we're given a handful of decades to figure out what it all means. We wake up, we grow, we love, we fall, we hope. And if we're honest, it mostly feels confusing, disorienting, and meaningless.

This is why humanity reaches for God and religion. We're aware of our vulnerability and need something greater to anchor us. We need something big enough to hold our fears and our suffering. We cling to scriptures and teachings that offer us direction and comfort. We hold on to the verses because they remind us that we matter.

Yet, even with religion to anchor us, we forget and lose our way.

We know what we're supposed to do to live right. We know the better path. We know the truth. Yet we still do the complete opposite. We promise ourselves we'll change. We swear we won't fall back into the same patterns. And then, somehow, we do. Again. And again. And again.

Our lack of discipline, willpower, or consistency slams us headfirst into the wall of shame.

We cry in frustration. We beat ourselves up for getting it wrong for the thousandth time. We hate ourselves for failing again after promising to do better. We wonder what's wrong with us. *Why can't I get it together? Why do I keep making the same mistakes?*

This struggle is universal, but it doesn't unite us. It isolates us.

Instead of drawing closer to one another, we hide. We pretend. We cover up the parts of ourselves we're afraid won't be accepted. We build up walls, hoping our stained souls won't be noticed. We hide from others, ourselves, and from God.

But hiding is never God's will. Hiding isn't rooted in Love.

You Must Remember

Here's what I want you to remember, maybe more than

anything else in this book: You were never meant to live under the crushing weight of perfection.

God isn't shocked by your humanity. He isn't asking for you to be perfect, because He remembers how you were made. He remembers that you're dust. He knows you're flesh awakening to the Divine. A child learning to walk. A soul returning to Love.

Judgment isn't hanging over your head, waiting for you to fail again. That judgment died on the cross with Jesus. What remains is Love, and Love is mercy, patience, and compassion. A steady Presence that doesn't recoil when you stumble.

So when you forget and slip back into your old habits, old fears, old ways of being, don't turn on yourself with a whip.

Instead, remember and return to Love.

Return to Love

Forgetting doesn't mean you're failing God. It means you're human. Your weakness doesn't disqualify you. No, it's the very place divine Love meets you.

When you wake up lost on a forgotten road, simply realign your mind with Love, and you're back on the right path. Instantly. Fully. With no need to give your forgetfulness another thought.

This is what forgiveness looks like.

Not a one-time event, but a continual returning home. A daily dying to the old self and choosing, again and again, to build from the ground up. You'll do this not seven times, but seventy times seven. And even then, you haven't arrived.

Salvation isn't a finish line you cross. It's a life you build. Stone by stone.

You're not too late, and you haven't missed the mark. You're exactly where you are meant to be. No matter how many times you get off course, or forget, or lose your way, you're always standing in the center of the infinite sea of Love. With every breath you take, you're participating in something sacred. Every time you remember and recenter, you're laying another stone in your cathedral.

This is Your Offering

Expanding your life into something abundant is your offering.

It's your gift back to the One who gave it. It's a gift to those who came before you, and a shelter for those who will come after. Your life is yours to build, but it was never yours to keep. You're a traveler passing through, entrusted with something precious for a brief moment in time.

Don't hide. Don't bury yourself beneath the earth. Never dim your light because you're afraid it isn't perfect. Don't shrink your cathedral because someone else's looks bigger or brighter.

The world doesn't need another flawless social feed. It needs your courage to create something with meaning, no matter how imperfect it is. It needs your willingness to keep building even when your hands are bloody and your vision is blurry.

Shine into the darkness because Love lives within you. Build boldly because you trust the One supporting you.

You were made for such a time as this. You were made for this life and this work.

Pick up your chisel.

Return to Love, and begin again.
And again.
And again.

AFFIRMATION

"I will return to Love."

ANTHEM OF THE LIVING CATHEDRAL

Oh, that you may come to know the God
Who dwells within the holiest of holy places.

You will not find Him in chapels built by human hands.
He's not in relics, hymns, or wooden altars.
He's not in Sunday mornings, padded pews, or sermons from
a pulpit.

His temple is nearer than your next breath.
It's not built of stone and marble,
But molded of flesh and bone, of mind and spirit.
You are His sacred temple.

He chose you as His dwelling place,
The altar where Love burns eternal.
Every heartbeat is a hymn.

Every word is a prayer.
Every breath, an offering.

Bend low, take off your shoes
For where you stand is holy.
It's not the earth that's sacred, but you.
You are the holy ground.

Now the work begins.
You are on this earth to expand in Love,
To build from the kingdom within.

To enter, you must leave the world of loaves and fishes.
You cannot see, taste, or touch the kingdom.
It's only through the inner chamber
Of your mind that you can enter.

It's from this hidden temple,
From this secret place,
That you fulfill your purpose
And do God's will.

Pick up your chisel,
Pick up your hammer,
You were made for a time such as this,
To build your holy offering.

Do not hide your light.
Do not dim your spark.
Do not bury yourself in the earth.
But build on the mountaintop.

You are His light.
You are His temple.
You are His dwelling place.

Rise now, beloved,
Look to the sky,
For you are building a cathedral.

ACKNOWLEDGMENTS

To my husband, Matt, thank you for your endless patience and encouragement through all the years when I said I would write this book and didn't. You're the best coach ever!

To my children, Charis, Porter, Hunter, and Christian, you motivate me to pursue my dreams more than you'll ever know. I hope my life inspires you to do the same thing. Go and build amazing lives.

To my MoM and dad, thank you for believing in the vision for my life long before I did. MoM, your faith in me has always been the soil where my dreams could take root.

To my in-laws, your support has meant more than you know. Mom, thank you for your gentle nudges to keep writing what's in my heart.

To my best friend, Christy, I wrote the * book! We did it. Thank you for listening to every idea, cheering me on every time I started…again, and always reminding me that this dream was worth finishing.

To my Manifesting Abundance group, this book was birthed from our 60-day challenges. You're the OG cathedral builders.

To my Beta Reader Book Club, Anna-Colby, Lauren, Bonnie, Christy, Anamaye, Charis, MoM, and Jessica. Thank you for taking the time to read this draft and offer your feedback. It means so much.

To Love, You thrill me more and more every day. Thank You for allowing me to live and move and have my being in You.

ABOUT THE AUTHOR

Charity Craig is an international marriage coach, writer, and spiritual teacher featured in publications such as *Good Morning America*, *People*, *The Huffington Post*, and Australia's *Take Five Magazine*. Through her courses and one-on-one coaching, she's spent the past decade helping thousands of women heal and rebuild their marriages.

Today, Charity's work extends beyond marriage into the broader spiritual principles of inner healing, divine Love, and personal transformation. Her life's work is to help people heal from their wounds and awaken to their potential so that they may live the abundant life they were created to live.

Charity and her husband, Matt, are building their dream life in the countryside with their four teenagers, two dogs, and a flock of chickens.

For more information:
charitycraig.com
charity@charitycraig.com

ALSO BY CHARITY CRAIG

I'm Building a Cathedral Notebook

28 Days of Inner Healing

Forgiveness After Betrayal